The apostle Paul wrote to the church of Corinth and said:

> Are we beginning to praise ourselves again? Are we like others, who need to bring you letters of recommendation, or who ask you to write such letters on their behalf? Surely not! The only letter of recommendation we need is you yourselves. Your lives are a letter written in our hearts; everyone can read it and recognize our good work among you (2 Corinthians 3:1–2 NLT).

It is common for a book to have a list of endorsements. I could ask a bunch of celebrity pastors who do not know me to write something flattering about this book. I think the best endorsements come from people who have already been using the *Promise Principle*™ in a group or in their own study. Here are several responses from men and women like that:

> God brought this principle into my life in a time when I almost lost my family. God's grace saved me. I am learning to put Jesus first in my life and not let the circumstances of this world control me. I am learning to walk with God through His Word and truly *live*, rather than run from Him and die.
> — Christian Danobeytia

> Doing the *Promise Principle* taught me to dive into passages that I would have normally glanced over. The Lord has

revealed things I didn't even realize I needed to hear. This study technique encourages me to take even the simplest verse and find what He wants me to discover in it. — Rebekah Dolan

As a first-year student in high school, I was introduced to the *Promise Principle*. Through engaging in it, I learned to "escape[d] the corruption in this world caused by evil desires" (2 Peter 1:4 NIV). This set me on a path of going against the grain of the culture, influencing my whole life. It changed my intentions daily to seek His kingdom first. I grew so hungry to read the Bible and pray, and with that my relationship with the Lord became so intimate. Using the *Promise Principle* helped me through many trials in high school; it laid a foundation of knowing the character of God and the promises He has kept and will always keep. I know I can trust Him. — Sarah Larson

The Lord has given Phillip some of the most incredible insights on what it means to live a transformed life by God's Word! I have prayed the promises of God since I was in high school, but after reading Phillip's book I now know how to respond to the promises of God with my spirit, so that I am led by the Spirit of God rather than overwhelmed with my feelings and circumstances. Whether you're a high school student or preparing for retirement, this book, when you apply what it teaches, will change your life. It definitely has changed mine. — Matt Hunter

"I don't understand the Bible." "The Bible is too big, I don't know where to start." "This doesn't apply to me." All of these are phrases I hear when students begin reading the Bible for the first time. The *Promise Principle* allows me to teach them how to pray, read God's Word for themselves, and fight the lies of the enemy with the truth. I hear time and time again from students how this has changed their life. God's Word is immutable, infallible, and eternal, and the *Promise Principle* is the most effective method to help anyone grasp the Word of God and apply it! I guarantee it will radically impact the way you read God's Word too! — Maddie Smith

The world we live in has tragically lost its ability to connect, yet this is what it yearns for above all else. The *Promise Principle* has allowed me to connect all whom I pastor—my family, young adults, business professionals, congregants who are hurting, empty nesters, and males and females alike—to the only One worth connecting to. — Matt Lankenau

Being in a *Promise Principle* group has been truly eye-opening and transformative. Each week I come away with a new nugget of truth or promise, even if I've read the passage a hundred times before. This way of studying the Word has also enhanced my personal quiet times. The Lord is showing me more and more of His Word each day. — Katie Smith

Being part of a *Promise Principle* group has helped me to become vulnerable, not only with other men but also vulnerable with my wife, which has strengthened and continues to strengthen our marriage. I wasn't comfortable praying at all; however, the group helped me to grow in that area through activating God's promises for us. I am now praying in those promises with my wife and kids. — Marc Whitcomb

This is the best discipleship process I have ever seen to help men and women learn how to hear from God, persevere under trial, and become the spiritual leaders of their homes. I highly recommend this book to pastors who are looking for depth in the hearts of their people through a process that is simple, duplicatable, and sustainable. — Todd McIntyre

My husband and I lead a couples *Promise Principle* group and it is amazing! Everyone is excited and participates. Some have never looked at Scripture in this way or prayed Scripture out loud. I am blown away at how powerful this is. I've led hundreds of groups in the past, and I've never seen such intimacy and vulnerability happen by just using Scripture. There is something powerful when couples begin declaring the truths of the Word, thanking the Lord for His blessings, and praying Scriptures out loud. — Kristine Kemp

I believe the *Promise Principle* has helped me and so many others break through the barrier to studying God's Word independently and consistently. This method provides immediate life application, connection with others, and a prayerful examination of Scripture. It truly is life changing. — David Rische

The *Promise Principle* has opened my eyes to the many promises and commands in God's Word that previously remained hidden. Promises—truths and commands—that have the power to change the way I encounter and address the daily struggles life throws my way. This is a "principle" that I "promise" will have a profound impact on your spiritual life. — Coby Duffer

I have used *Promise Principle* on my own and in a small group. This is a great tool because it encourages us to look at Scripture in a new way. It is such a wonderful thing to gather around the table with a group of friends and not only read or look over a passage, but also search out the many promises God gives us in His Word and then apply a particular promise to our lives. Praying out that promise in a group, knowing others are standing with you, is a powerful exercise. As women, many times when we come together, we share our struggles and blessings, but using *Promise Principle* brings God's Word front and center as the foundation on which we stand. I would strongly recommend *Promise Principle* for individual and group study. — Tammy Williams

God still speaks! The *Promise Principle* allows guys to be real men and express their true hearts and feelings by reading the

Bible. Each word in the Bible has a practical life application. Since being in a *Promise Principle* group, I have been slow to anger and more aware of God's presence in my life. Thank you for the freedom. — Michael Garza

The *Promise Principle* has changed my life. I now read my Bible with more purpose than ever before. This has helped me gain a better understanding of who God is and what He has in store for my life. I'm learning to take my knowledge of God's promises to the next level by allowing them to affect my daily actions. — Michael Messer

The *Promise Principle* has taught me that God's Word has supplied me with everything I need to live a life of worship and faith. Due to the principle, I have been able to fully understand who God is and what He has done for me. The *Promise Principle* has now been integrated into my whole life from school, to the small group I lead, and my relationships with others. I am able to know truly who God is, which lets me live my life like Jesus. — Katy Duke

THE PROMISE PRINCIPLE

A NEW WAY TO ENCOUNTER THE BIBLE

PHILLIP HUNTER

To my parents, Phil and Roni Hunter
I dedicate this book you. You always taught me
there was "no substitute for obedience."
You have modeled a life lived by principle,
rather than by your circumstances.
Thank you for your faithfulness. I love you both.

Contents

Foreword

All authority in heaven and earth has been given to Me. Therefore, go and make disciples of all nations, baptizing them in the name of the Father, and of the Son and of the Holy Spirit, teaching them to obey everything I have commanded you. And surely I am with you always, to the very end of the age (Matthew 28:18–20 NIV).

I have always been enamored with the fact that this was one of the last commands Jesus gave to His disciples right before He ascended into heaven. As a young minister, I remember thinking that if these were some of Jesus' last words, then I better be about getting this done. I set out on a journey to figure out what that actually means. We all know that a disciple is a student, but Jesus made it clear that we are supposed to be making disciples that obey His teachings. As I would talk with many men who have been in ministry for some time, most of them would tell me that discipleship to them was teaching a class lasting from 6 to 52 weeks, which gave people enough information to learn how to follow Jesus. But what I was finding was that even though many of these people had a lot of information, they still struggled to follow Jesus when the circumstances in their lives became difficult.

As the men's pastor of Gateway Church in Southlake, Texas, I was given the task of discipling the men of our church. I wanted to create a process of discipleship that wasn't simply transferring information, but a spiritual transformation. After talking with many other pastors through the years, I was convinced that discipleship could not happen in a normal classroom format. We had to design something that wasn't just information but relationship driven. I felt like the men in our church needed role models or mentors (like Jesus) who they could not only learn from, but also relate to. We started what I called Project Mentor, where spiritually immature men would be connected to more spiritually mature mentors who would spend at least an hour a week building relationships and talking about Jesus's teachings and how to walk according to them. This process seemed to start off well. Without any marketing or advertising, I had about 35 mentors relating to over 75 men each week. As men started to hear about what we were doing, I had another 150 men ask if they could get involved in this process and start meeting with a mentor. The dilemma I faced was that I didn't have enough mentors to go around, and we had over 10,000 men in our church who probably would never get connected to this process due to the amount of time that it took and the limited number of mentors I could recruit and train. I felt stuck for about eight months. I didn't know how I would be able to reach the numbers of men who needed and wanted spiritual support.

It was during this time that my pastor, Robert Morris, gave me permission to recruit a larger staff for the men and bring in a discipleship pastor to help us grow this area of our ministry. We called Pastor Phillip Hunter to do just that, but I told him that I wanted him to learn how we disciple at Gateway and figure out a way to raise up more mentors to solve our dilemma. After about two weeks, during my quiet time I felt the Lord tug on my heart that I was to give Phillip permission to not only run our discipleship process, but also to change it and do what he thought necessary. However, I was a bit resistant to do this. I felt that if I allowed Pastor Phillip to lead another way, he would probably come up with a solution that followed the typical classroom format with very little relationship building and not much transformation. So, following what I took as orders from God, I reluctantly told Pastor Phillip with my teeth clenched that he had my permission to revamp our discipleship process *but* it had to be good. He laughed and said, "Let me pray about it for the next couple of weeks and I will get back to you."

Two weeks later, Pastor Phillip was back in my office with what he thought would be a supplement to Project Mentor, but instead of one-on-one discipleship it would look more like a group format. Trying to be open minded, I listened to his proposal as he explained to me what he called the *Promise Principle* based on 2 Peter 1:3–11, which is what Peter taught to his followers about how to grow in their relationship with Christ. Phillip explained what discipleship was and what it wasn't and told me that the reason men have a hard time following the teachings of Christ is because they don't know how to take the promises of God from their head to their spirit. I had never heard that before and I was very curious. Then before we launched our first *Promise Principle* group, I asked him to lead our small staff of men's ministers through the process.

I remember that first day. As with most men, when forced to learn something new or do something required by their boss, there was a little resistance. Pastor Phillip explained the process and off we went. Within minutes of launching this study, I had men in my office not only emotional but with tears in their eyes as they received the promises of God in the circumstances they were dealing with personally. I was amazed by their reactions, and how emotional I felt as I read passages from Ephesians that I had read many times before but was now praying them over my circumstances. As soon as that first meeting was over, I knew why God nudged me that day—He had a different plan to reach the men of our church, and we could do this faster and simpler through the *Promise Principle*. Immediately, we laid down Project Mentor and started to build *Promise Principle* groups on all six of our campuses at Gateway Church. In the last two years, over 90 groups of men, teenagers, women, and married couples have been launched. We have also seen other churches take this model and heard incredible testimonies about how it has impacted their members. I believe these are the most productive groups I have ever been a part of in my 27 years of ministry.

Let me give you an example of how powerful this technique is for helping people encounter the Word of God. A few of weeks ago, a man in our church asked if I would meet with him because he was struggling with his faith. He had told me that his wife was a lot stronger in her faith than he was and that he thought he might even be agnostic. He wanted to feel the things his wife did about God. He said his whole life he had been in church, but he was having a hard time believing. In his own words, he said that he leaned toward a more scientific approach to life. If he couldn't see or touch something, then he really couldn't believe it. I met with him at a local coffee shop, and after hearing his story, I asked if he would be willing to read a few Scriptures with me and learn how to read the Bible in a different way. I could tell he thought I was trying to sell Christianity to him, but he was willing to let me walk him through a few things. I told him to underline any promise he read in the first six verses of Ephesians chapter 1, and then we would talk about them when we finished reading. I noticed he underlined a few verses, so I asked him why he did that. Sarcastically, he said, "Because you told me to." I said, "I know, but why that one?" Then he told me about a circumstance he was having with his faith and how he thought this one particular Scripture related to that circumstance. I said, "Great. Now I want you to pray that Scripture out loud over your life." He said, "Right now?" I said, "Yes." After looking around to see if anyone would hear him pray, he closed his eyes and prayed the Scripture he had under-lined. Immediately, his eyes filled with tears. As soon as he finished, I asked him what he was feeling, and he said, "Emotional." I said, "That is what your wife feels when she reads the Bible too." Suddenly, his countenance started to change. I asked him again what he was think-ing. He replied, "I have read the Bible many times and for the first time I read it with my spirit." I said, "That is how God intended you to read it all along." I invited him to a group that I was facilitating the next day, and he said he would come.

That next day, we were reading 2 Corinthians 5 as a group. He had underlined a promise and asked to respond to it in prayer. Immediately, during his prayer, he started to get emotional again. After his prayer, I said to him that it sure was funny for a guy who was questioning his faith yesterday, who never gets emotional about God, for the two times he prayed Scriptures over his life to feel so emotional. He started to laugh and said, "I have never known God like this before."

What you are about to read is a principle that isn't from a church or another book, but it is right out of the teachings of the apostle Peter. I am convinced that Jesus taught Peter this principle in the three and a half years he was with Him. Regardless of what you think about God, He wants you to live in peace and joy no matter what circumstances you are going through in your life. I know that if you will apply this principle to your life, you will never be the same. I pray that God will do in you what He is doing in my life and the lives of so many other men and women across our church.

—Todd McIntyre, Pastor, Gateway Church

Acknowledgments

I have been so richly blessed and want to say thank you to several people.

First, to my beautiful wife, Shelly, I couldn't imagine life without you—thank you for being my biggest cheerleader. I love you. To my five children, Atley, Avery, Canon, Champ, and Jubilee—you are God's greatest gifts to me and the best part of me. To my parents—thank you for teaching me to hide God's Word in my heart. To my brothers, Josh and Matt—I had the best childhood because of you. I love you both and I pray for you every day. To my "In-Loves," Rob and Susie Ruth—thank you for giving me the greatest gift you could give me in your daughter, and for the love and support you continually give us all.

I want to thank John Andersen and Craig Dunnagan from Gateway Publishing for giving me a chance to write. I never thought I could write a paper longer than 10 pages in college. Thank you, John, for poring over these pages, your late nights, and making sure everything was just right. To Gateway Church, I love this house. My heart overflows with gratefulness every time I walk into the building. To Byron Copeland, thank you for inviting me here and letting God use you to open the doors. To Todd McIntrye, thank you for empowering me to do what the Lord had put in me to do. The world is getting this principle because you said, "Yes." To the team that pushed our *Promise Principle* groups—Jonathan McNabb, Dustin Herron, James Lee, Chris Griffin, Doyle Duran, Josh Briscoe, Matt Lankenau, Matt Osgood, Justin Greene, Jason Settle, and Dustin Sample, I love working with you all.

I also want to thank Pastor Robert Morris. Thank you for letting me to do this book under the banner of Gateway Church. In all my hurts, God has used the health and purity of Gateway Church, its staff, and its people to see what the church is supposed to be. I am grateful for your heart for not only our local church, but also God's church around the world.

Introduction

Have you ever done something a certain way your entire life, and then someone teaches you a different way to do it and you are amazed? For example, I have a technique to get the extra grease out of meat: I tilt the skillet sideways with the lid atop the skillet, letting the grease run out the crack. The problem is that I can't get all the grease, or a little meat falls out of the skillet. Then one day my mother saw me doing this, and she said, "Oh, honey, let me show you another technique that is much simpler and more effective." She grabbed a couple of paper towels, folded them a few times, and then just dabbed the meat with the towels. Suddenly, there was no grease in the skillet. She threw the paper towels into the trash and said, "See, it's that simple!" I was amazed. There wasn't any meat on the counter, and there was no more grease in the pan. My mother didn't tell me my way was wrong. She simply showed me a different technique that has changed the way I cook.

That is what I want to do—I want to show you a new technique to study the Bible based on something I call the *Promise Principle*. I define the *Promise Principle* as "God's fundamental way to disciple believers through His promises so that we won't participate in our old nature, but participate in His *divine nature*." What is our old nature? Simply put, you live according to how you feel and think. Those thoughts and feelings are always dictated by the circumstances of life, whether they are troubles or temptations. Once you are saved, your spirit comes to life, and the process of growing in Christ is learning to obey God's Spirit. The apostle Peter says that God has given us His promises, and if we respond, we can actually participate in His *divine nature* (2 Peter 1:4).

I am not telling you another way is wrong, but the technique you will learn in this book has changed the way I and many people read the Bible. Many of us know we need to be discipled but have never had someone give us a specific technique to help us grow in spiritual maturity. I will teach you how to respond to the promises of God while helping you engage your spirit to lead your soul. I will teach you what I believe Jesus meant when He told His disciples that they need to teach followers of Christ to obey everything He commanded.

This book will teach you how we lead and facilitate a *Promise Principle* group. You will see what it means to use the Bible as your curriculum and let the Holy Spirit be your teacher. I have been discipling people for over twenty years, and I have never seen a faster or more profound way of putting God's Word in a person's heart so that their mind can be transformed.

Most discipleship courses I have encountered in both church and parachurch ministries are based on curricula. Before you read this book, I want you to know this not a curriculum. It is simply an explanation or technique to guide you as you study the Word of God. The goal is to help you internalize the Word. The Bible says in James 4:7 that we are to submit to God, resist the devil, and he will flee. If the Word of God isn't *in you*, you will not be able to submit to it so you can resist the devil.

I am excited that you picked up this book. I pray that it will change the way you look at growing and maturing as a Christian. I pray it will help you see the difference between just having Bible knowledge as information in your head, and letting your soul be transformed by receiving the truth of God's promises into your heart. I pray it will empower and encourage you not only to read the Word of God for yourself, but also to equip you to lead a Bible study to encourage others. And most importantly, I pray it will teach you how to hear God speak to you through His Word and through prayer.

I am a simple person and I think simply. I believe God's Word and His ways are simpler than we usually try to make them. I pray God will allow you to understand every word you read with clarity and, more than anything, that you see the treasure of God's Word and God's plan for you to grow in spiritual maturity.

Responding to the Promises of God,
Phillip Hunter

1

Three Parts of You

The last day of my junior year in high school, I decided to go to the river with a group of my friends. Our intentions weren't to go fishing, but to find a lot of mud and take our four-wheel-drive trucks for a ride. I didn't own a car myself, so on this particular day, I rode with my friend in his Toyota 4x4 truck. Four or five other vehicles joined us for this off-roading excursion. But for my story, the most important vehicle belonged to my best friend's girlfriend. She owned a jeep and he drove it while his girlfriend sat in the front passenger seat.

We started driving the vehicles through the mud. Then, at some point, all of us proceeded down a muddy trail with a big ravine down one side of it. One truck fishtailed on the trail, but made it safely past the ravine. However, the jeep that my best friend was driving also fishtailed, and he wasn't able to straighten the vehicle. The jeep slid off the trail and down into the ravine. The ravine was at least 20 to 25 feet deep (about 6 to

8 meters). The drop didn't harm the jeep or my friends, but once they reached the bottom the vehicle was stuck. Mud covered the jeep and its tires sunk so deep that we could barely see the top of each wheel.

It never occurred to us to go for help, because our teenage brains couldn't process that it was the smart thing to do. So, we began to make matters worse, mainly because we didn't want to get in trouble with our parents. First, we collected tree branches, sticks, and anything else we could find to push down under the tires for traction. Then, somehow, I found myself sitting in the driver's seat. This detail is important, because my parents had a rule that we were never to drive another person's car. However, I thought to myself, "This is different—my friends really need my help." I devised what I thought was the right plan to free the jeep from this trap. I decided to rock the jeep back and forth by repeatedly alternating between first gear and reverse. I thought I could slowly build momentum to shoot the jeep up the ravine and back onto the trail.

I was right ... at least partly. We followed my plan and then the jeep shot up the slope with the tires slipping and sliding. Just as I neared the crest, I ran out of traction and the tires began to spin. I thought, "All I need is few more feet." So I let my foot off the gas and let the jeep slide down the hill again. I reasoned that I was so close to the top on my first attempt that all I needed to do was to go full throttle on my next run. Then the jeep would be free.

I prepared for my second attempt, but when I hit the gas, something made a loud pop. Seconds later, smoke billowed from the engine. My friends began shouting, "Fire!" I jumped out of the vehicle. Only then did I see little fireballs dropping into the mud from the engine compartment. In terror, I scrambled to the top of the ravine and away from the jeep. My friends and I stood helpless, watching as the whole engine burst into flames. Explosions followed, and the entire vehicle convulsed. Strangely, it felt almost like we were in a movie. But if a camera had been rolling, it would have captured eight teenage boys standing helplessly with their mouths wide open and one teenage girl sobbing.

The story didn't end there. The police and firetrucks arrived. My parents arrived and my summer vacation began and ended within less than two hours. There would be consequences for our actions. My dad gave a stern lecture. I don't remember all of the contents, but I never forgot one of his favorite questions: "What were you thinking?" I attempted to give a lame excuse; I tried to tell him why I felt that I needed to break the rule about driving other people's vehicles in this one situation. He wasn't buying it. He stopped me and said, "Son, we do not live our lives based on circumstances. We live our lives based on principles."

> "Son, we do not live our lives based on circumstances. We live our lives based on principles."

I had heard that statement many times from my parents, but at that moment, it became painfully relevant. Its truth leapt into my heart and became a life statement for me: "Live by principles, not by circumstances." Every day, that statement challenges me as I live and grow as a person. It isn't my nature, however. In fact, it is my human nature to live according to my circumstances. This nature is sinful at its core. But I don't have to live that way ... and neither do you.

In the Image of God

Then God said, "Let us make man in our image, after our likeness. And let them have dominion over the fish of the sea and over the birds of the heavens and over the livestock and over all the earth and over every creeping thing that creeps on the earth."

So God created man in his own image,
in the image of God he created him;
male and female he created them (Genesis 1:26–27 ESV).

The apostle Paul says the whole world follows the same pattern (Ephesians 2). This pattern is to live according to our circumstances. All of us are born with a condition that causes us to follow the desires of our bodies and minds. The New Testament refers to this pattern as our "flesh," which results in our being "children of disobedience." We live this way because all of us are born with something dead inside of us.

The best way to understand this pattern is to go back to the beginning of creation. Genesis says that when God made man and woman, He created them in His image (Genesis 1:27). For example, God is eternal. If God created you in His image, then you are eternal. Ecclesiastes says, "He has planted eternity in the human heart" (Ecclesiastes 3:11 NLT). That is why there is always the feeling of loss when loved ones die, whether they are 8 years old or 80 years old. It never seems fair. The reason is that God did not wire us to die, but rather to live eternally.

God is relational, so He created us in His image with that same characteristic. The Bible describes a perfect relationship between the Father, Son, and Holy Spirit. God is intimate and engaged. As His relational created beings, He made us to know and be known. Jesus says that the two greatest commandments are to love God and to love people. The whole Law of God is based on those two things (Matthew 22:36–40).

Everything we do revolves around relationships. For example, when most teenagers wake up and head to school, they don't think about what great things they are going to learn in algebra or biology. Instead, they think about the other teens who they are going to see and those who might see them. When people go shopping, they aren't thinking, "I really need to find some materials to protect myself from the elements outside." They do it for the purpose of relationships and who might see them in their new clothes. What do prisons do with inmates who need further discipline? They put them in solitary confinement. Since God created us for relationship, the loss of human connection has a profound effect on us.

One of the most important aspects of God making us in His image is that we are three in one, which is much like God. The Bible teaches that God is triune: Father, Son, and Holy Spirit. In a similar way, the Bible teaches that we have body, soul, and spirit. The body isn't hard to understand because we can see it. However, many people get confused about Scripture's references to the soul and the spirit. These two must be different, because they can be divided (Hebrews 4:12).

Your soul consists of your mind, will, and emotions. Some readers will be familiar with soul music, a type of music that originated in the 1950s and 1960s. This music elicits strong emotions; it was actually a combination of rhythm and blues and gospel. Music conveys the deepest passions and desires of the human heart. These things make up your soul.

Your spirit is the eternal part of you. When God created Adam, He blew the breath of life into Adam's nostrils (Genesis 2:7). God wasn't performing CPR. He was breathing spirit life into Adam. God designed each human to have a body, a soul, and a spirit. The most important part of Adam was his spirit. That spirit separated humans from every other living thing in God's creation. God designed us in such a way that our spirits would lead us and allow us to relate to God. Jesus referred to this truth when He said, "God *is* Spirit, and those who worship Him must worship in spirit and truth" (John 4:24 NKJV).

Do you recall the story of Adam and Eve in the garden? God told them if they ate from the Tree of Knowledge of Good and Evil, they would immediately die. When you read the story, they don't seem to die when they eat the tree's fruit. However, they really did die. Even though they didn't immediately die physically, their spirits did. What "fell" that day was the spirit of every human. The outcome was our fallen, sinful nature. Consequently, every single person is born with a dead spirit. So now, instead of our spirits leading us, every person follows the world's pattern, which is under the control of the body and soul (Ephesians 2).

In fact, that is why God had to remove Adam and Eve from the garden. God expelled them so they wouldn't reach out and eat from the Tree of Life—if they did, then they would live forever (Genesis 3:22–23). Why didn't God want them to eat from the Tree of Life anymore? They could have eaten from it earlier, but not after disobeying God. It wasn't that God didn't want them to live forever; God had created them to do that. However, God knew it would be horrible for them to live forever in this fallen condition with a dead spirit. God's mercy and love removed them from the garden. Man could not live eternally without being renewed.

> So now, instead of our spirits leading us, every person follows the world's pattern, which is under the control of the body and soul (Ephesians 2).

Circumstances

And you were ***dead [your spirit]*** in the trespasses and sins in which you once walked, following the course of this world, following the prince of the power of the air, the spirit that is now at work in the sons of disobedience—among whom we all once lived in the passions of our flesh, carrying out the desires of *the body and the mind [soul],* and were by nature children of wrath, like the rest of mankind (Ephesians 2:1–3 ESV emphasis added).

Every person is born with a body, a soul, and a dead spirit. The whole world follows the same pattern, led by their bodies and souls. But where are they leading? They take us where our feelings and thoughts tell us to go. Your body feels, and your soul both feels and thinks. But what controls how we think and feel? *Circumstances.* Your circumstances will always influence the way you feel and think.

Two types of circumstances usually rule our bodies and souls: *troubles and temptations.* Troubles include financial problems, health issues, and relationship struggles. Perhaps a doctor tells you that you have a disease. Or maybe you can't find a job, so you don't know how you are going to pay your mortgage. Or you are suffering from a broken relationship with your spouse, parent, or child. I am sure you are facing some kind of trouble as you read this. Troubles try to rule your feelings and thoughts. If you allow them to do so, they will fill you with fear, worry, anxiety, and other negative thoughts and emotions.

> Your circumstances will always influence
> the way you feel and think.

James says, "Temptation comes from our own desires, which entice us and drag us away" (James 1:14 NLT). Paul says, "The temptations in your life are no different from what others experience" (1 Corinthians 10:13 NLT). Temptations entice you to feel or think that something is good in the moment. They promise fulfillment but if we yield to them they lead to regrets and negative consequences.

I confess that I love junk food. However, even though I have an appetite for it, eating it always leads to regrets because I don't feel well later. Eve's appetite peaked in the garden. Genesis says that when she saw the fruit was good for eating, she took it and ate it (Genesis 3:6). God did not tell her that is was good for her to eat. Instead, through temptation, she was enticed to think it was good for her and would fulfill her needs. Unlike when I eat junk food, Eve got more than a bellyache. Her consequence was death. James continues by saying that wrongful desires "give birth to sinful actions. And when sin is allowed to grow, it gives birth to death" (James 1:15 NLT).

Troubles and temptation rob us of the feeling of peace. The Old Testament's word for "peace," *Shalom*, actually means "wholeness." Peace is feeling complete, lacking nothing. Often we think if our circumstances would change or go away, everything would be better. We want to be whole—in our health, finances, and relationships. If we are whole in those areas, we think we will be happy. That is how the enemy wants us to think, but it isn't true.

We don't plan to let our circumstances rule us; we all want to live by principles or beliefs. But we can't. By ourselves, we don't have the ability. The apostle Paul writes about this problem. He laments about how miserable he is. He doesn't want to do the things he does, and he cannot do the things he wants to do. Circumstances always drive his sinful nature. He has no hope. He is doomed like the rest of the world (Romans 7).

Paul's problem is common to all of us. People follow their feelings and thoughts. That is the pattern of the whole world. Think about your own life. How often do you let your thoughts dictate what you do, rather than let the principles of God's Word guide your action? How often do you stop following God's Word because your circumstances change your feelings? You know you should forgive someone, but you don't. Is it because you don't feel like it yet? You think if people really knew how much that person hurt you, they would understand why you couldn't forgive. You are living by your circumstances. However, as Paul writes, "Thank God! The answer is in Jesus Christ our Lord" (Romans 7:25 NLT).

God Knows Spiritual CPR

> But God, being rich in mercy, because of the great love with which he loved us, even when we were dead in our trespasses, made us **alive** together with Christ (Ephesians 2:4–5a ESV emphasis added).

When God made us alive together in Christ Jesus, which part did He make alive? It's our spirit. Paul says that something happens when we change our hearts and minds, turn from our sin, and confess Jesus as Lord of our lives. Paul says it this way: "The Spirit of God, who raised Jesus from the dead, lives in you. And just as God raised Christ Jesus from the dead, he will give life to your mortal bodies by this same Spirit living within you" (Romans 8:11 NLT). It was the Holy Spirit who entered the tomb and raised Jesus from the dead. In the same way, the Holy Spirit enters the tomb of your mortal body, resurrects your dead spirit, and brings it back to life.

Furthermore, if God resurrects our dead spirits and saves us, then why would we think that our good work could save us? How many church services must we attend? How many good deeds must we perform for our dead spirits to be resurrected? Paul "was a member of the Pharisees, who demand the strictest obedience to the Jewish law" (Philippians 3:5 NLT), a man other Jews would consider morally righteous, That is why Jesus said that if Nicodemus wanted to be saved, he would have to be born of the Spirit and not just of his mother (John 3:1–7).

God blew the "breath of life" into Adam's nostrils. The "breath of life" appears again when Jesus stands before His disciples after the resurrection (John 20:22). He breathed on them and said, "Receive the Holy Spirit." Imagine how this scene may have happened. Jesus appears before His disciples, opens His mouth, and makes a loud exhaling sound. This act may seem unusual, but it was incredibly life changing for these men. As a result, these men's spirits were no longer dead. They were as alive as Adam and Eve before they ate from the Tree of Knowledge of Good and Evil.

> It was the Holy Spirit who entered the tomb and raised Jesus from the dead. In the same way, the Holy Spirit enters the tomb of your mortal body, resurrects your dead spirit, and brings it back to life.

And [He] raised us up with him and seated us with him in the heavenly places in Christ Jesus, so that in the coming ages he might show the immeasurable riches of his grace in kindness toward us in Christ Jesus. For by grace you have been saved through faith. And this is not your own doing; it is the gift of God, not a result of works, so that no one may boast (Ephesians 2:6–9 ESV).

God makes us alive in Christ. Paul continues by saying that we are seated with Jesus in heavenly places. Much of what Paul writes about in Ephesians 2 is a mystery, but God is so serious about your salvation that He already sees your spirit seated in heaven. Then Paul says that you have been saved through faith. What about you has God saved? It is your spirit. The Greek word for saved, *sozo*, means "whole." How amazing! Earlier I wrote about how we often think our circumstances control our "wholeness." Salvation is wholeness! Robert Morris, the founding senior pastor of Gateway Church, says, "At the moment of salvation, your spirit is made whole. If God makes your spirit whole, then the Bible promises that one day He will make your body whole. And if those two things are true, you are in the process of your soul being made whole."

God's process for making your soul whole is through spiritual maturity. God has made your spirit alive since you received Christ as Lord, but feelings and thoughts still dictate and rule your life. So Paul says, "Do not conform to the pattern of this world, but be transformed by the renewing of your mind" (Romans 12:2 NIV). What is the pattern that we should avoid following? The pattern of this world is that we follow our bodies and souls. Our circumstances rule us. This situation must change for us as believers. Paul says we must become people "who no longer follow our sinful nature but instead follow the Spirit" (Romans 8:4 NLT). For this change to happen, a process of spiritual maturity must begin, which means our spirits must lead us rather than allowing our bodies and souls to lead us.

> "At the moment of salvation, your spirit is made whole. If God makes your spirit whole, then the Bible promises that one day He will make your body whole. And if those two things are true, you are in the process of your soul being made whole."

2

Because I Said So

I am the father of five children. I couldn't be more proud of my children—but they aren't perfect. In fact, it seems they often don't hear me very well. I know they don't have a hearing loss; the problem is with their hearts, not their ears. Listening doesn't have to do with just your ears, it has to do with your heart. If a heart is tender and attentive, it's amazing what it can hear.

> Listening doesn't have to do with just your ears, it has to do with your heart.

When I was young, my mom would call us children to dinner—multiple times. We sat in another room watching TV. After several calls and no response, my brothers and I would hear heavy footsteps and the sound of our father loosening his leather belt. Amazingly, we heard that sound! We would jump to our feet because we knew that danger was near. None of us wanted a spanking, and my dad knew that heart adjustments sometimes began with a belt on our backsides.

As I look back, I realize that I demonstrated a lack of love when I didn't respond to my mom's voice. I love to hear my children say, "I love you, Daddy," but my children truly communicate love when they listen to me. They demonstrate love when they trust me and obey, even though they might want to do something else. Our heavenly Father wants the same thing from us.

God told King Saul to destroy the people and livestock completely in a battle against the Amalekites. Then God told Samuel to visit the king because God knew Saul didn't have a listening heart. When Samuel arrived, he asked Saul to give account for his actions. The king proudly replied, "I have obeyed the voice of the Lord ... I have utterly destroyed the Amalekites" (1 Samuel 15:20 NKJV). But Samuel heard the bleating sounds of sheep. So he asked Saul about the sounds. Then Saul boasted that he intended to sacrifice them to God. However, Samuel responded by saying, "to obey is better than sacrifice." Finally, he told Saul that God would rip the kingdom away from him because of this disobedience (1 Samuel 15:22, 27).

Perhaps you think God was extreme when He punished Saul. After all, the king planned to be obedient and worship God in the future with a great sacrifice.

However, 99 percent obedience is 100 percent disobedience in God's eyes. How did Saul not hear God's command? God told him to destroy the Amalekites and all their belongings. Saul had a heart problem; that is why. He wasn't listening to God. Even though he was going to obey God eventually, he was still disobedient to God's precise command.

The Shema

> Hear, O Israel! The Lord our God, the Lord *is* one! You shall love the Lord your God with all your heart, with all your soul, and with all your strength (Deuteronomy 6:4–5 NKJV).

One of the most important passages of the Old Testament is the *Shema* in Deuteronomy 6. The title for this passage comes from its first word *Shema,* usually translated as "hear."[1] Jesus quoted this passage when the Pharisees attempted to trap Him by asking Him which commandment is the greatest (Matthew 22:37). The word, however, has a stronger meaning than simply to "hear." If a parent asks a child, "Do you hear me?" it is not a question about the child's auditory capabilities. Instead, the parent wants action; the parent wants the child to obey upon hearing. For God, hearing and

1. Chad Brand et al., eds., "Shema," *Holman Illustrated Bible Dictionary* (Nashville, TN: Holman Bible Publishers, 2003), 1481.

obeying aren't two separate concepts combined with a conjunction. To God, they are synonymous and inseparable. If you hear, you will obey. If you aren't obeying, it is because you aren't hearing.[2]

Then God adds another word to the other two—"love." This trio of words belongs together: "hear," "obey," and "love." The command to hear/obey is also the command to love God with your entire being. How do you love Him with everything? You hear Him in everything. You obey Him in everything. God spells love as *S-h-e-m-a*. Until you give everything to Him, you have been a child of disobedience (Ephesians 2:2). When you have obeyed the things you feel and think over your entire life, hearing and obeying God is a huge adjustment.

Did your father ever use the same four-word sentence that my dad did when he responded to me? At the time, I thought it was a weak line and it infuriated me. What was that sentence? *Because I said so.* I would ask permission to spend the night with a friend or ask to go out with my friends. And he would say, "No," but never give a reason for his response. Then I would ask, "Why not?" Then he would reply, "Because I said so." I am sure I stomped away and slammed a door more than once. Did you do something like that?

---

2. Gary Hardin, "Obedience," ed. Chad Brand et al., *Holman Illustrated Bible Dictionary* (Nashville, TN: Holman Bible Publishers, 2003), 1206.

> When you have obeyed the things you feel and think over your entire life, hearing and obeying God is a huge adjustment.

I love being a dad. My children are my dreams come true. Many of my thoughts are about how I can build them up, how I can help them experience all the best things, and how I can protect them from everything that might hurt them. I always think of how creative I can be in expressing my love for them. Often, I drive home from work thinking about how I can bless them. There is never a time when I think, "I'm really going to treat them badly tonight." In fact, I feel great disappointment when I have an idea to do something special for them, but an ugly attitude or a rebellious heart spoils our plans. Then I can't reward them. I have to discipline them instead.

Suppose that one day my daughter comes to me and asks if she can go out on a date with a boy, and I don't approve of him. At that moment, how will I explain to her all my prayers and hopes for her future? How will I explain to her why I object to her potential date? It will be difficult. So I will respond by saying, "No." She will reply by asking, "Why not?" And, of course, I will say, "Because I said so!"

Like most children, she will believe that is the worst reason she has ever heard. But if she can just understand that I am giving the most profound, loving response that I could ever give, she will know I am completely for her. If she can understand the depth of my love for her and that I would move heaven and earth for her, she will know I care about her ultimate happiness. If she can trust my love for her, she will know I am looking out for her best interests. If she can grasp all those things, she will be able to say, "Oh, Dad! I know your love for me, and because you say so, that is enough for me." Because she knows the depth of my love, it won't be a burden for her to obey me.

You may think I need to wake up and come back to reality. You're probably thinking that no teenage daughter has ever said that to her father. Nevertheless, isn't that what would happen if we put childish thoughts and reasoning behind us (1 Corinthians 13:11) and matured in our thinking with God? My children don't have the maturity yet to understand that when I am saying, "Because I said so," I am actually telling them I love them. As a father, I now understand that phrase my dad would say to me. It drove me crazy, but it was the strongest and most life-giving thing that he could have ever said.

Spiritual maturity happens when we believe that no matter what circumstances we face—all we need to hear is God say, "Because I said so." Our obedience is the right response to His love. As you grow in spiritual maturity, you will realize that everything God has commanded in His Word brings life and peace to you, so it is never a burden.

> Spiritual maturity happens when we believe that no matter what circumstances we face—all we need to hear is God say, "Because I said so."

Consider one more parenting illustration. When I was little, my parents lived in a mobile home park. We didn't have our own front yard or a driveway, so I rode my tricycle on the sidewalk in front of our home. For a three-year-old boy who wanted adventure, the sidewalk grew boring quickly. I only had to go back and forth a few times before I saw everything I was going to see. Even though my parents told me not to ride my tricycle in the street, I would look to see if they were watching me. If no one was looking, I rode into the street and headed into a world of endless possibilities. Of course, I had watchful parents, because I could never get far before they caught and scolded me.

My young heart thought they were ruining all my fun and that they did not understand how the open road was calling out to me. I thought they burdened me by not letting me ride in the street. I threw a tantrum when they wouldn't let me get my way.

However, I don't think that way anymore. As I have matured and grown, I realized that my parents gave me that command because they loved me and they wanted to protect me from being hurt or even killed. Is it surprising that I don't think like a little child anymore? I finally realized that it is good for a three-year-old to keep obeying this command. I even gave the same order to my children when they were little.

The apostle John says, "In fact, this is love for God: to keep his commands. And his commands are not burdensome" (1 John 5:3 NIV). If you love God, you love His commands, and you realize it is for your ultimate good despite what you might feel or think at the time. You may have considered many of God's commands as burdens, but as you mature in Christ, you will find the psalmist's words also to be your confession:

> Oh, how I love your instructions!
> I think about them all day long.
> Your commands make me wiser than my enemies,
> for they are my constant guide.
> Yes, I have more insight than my teachers,
> for I am always thinking of your laws.
> I am even wiser than my elders,

for I have kept your commandments.
I have refused to walk on any evil path,
    so that I may remain obedient to your word.
I haven't turned away from your regulations,
    for you have taught me well.
How sweet your words taste to me;
    they are sweeter than honey.
Your commandments give me understanding;
    no wonder I hate every false way of life.
Your word is a lamp to guide my feet
    and a light for my path.
I've promised it once, and I'll promise it again:
    I will obey your righteous regulations
(Psalm 119:97–106 NLT).

Do these verses ring true in your heart? If you are a disciple of Jesus, this Scripture will become the echo of your heart. In fact, it can measure your spiritual maturity. Do you struggle to obey the voice of the Lord? Are His commands burdensome or sweeter than honey? For a disciple of Jesus, there is no substitute for obedience to God. This teaching is part of the Great Commission:

Teach these new disciples to obey all the commands I have given you (Matthew 28:20a NLT).

3

The Promise Principle

Therefore, go and make disciples of all the nations, baptizing them in the name of the Father and the Son and the
Holy Spirit. Teach these new disciples to obey all the commands I have given you. And be sure of this: I am with you
always, even to the end of the age. (Matthew 28:19–20 NLT).

Jesus commissioned the church to go into all the
world and make disciples. Disciples are people
who adhere to the teachings of another. They take
up the ways of someone else. Disciples of Jesus
learn from Him in order to live like Him; they follow
Him. What did Jesus model? He never lived by what
He felt and thought. He always obeyed His Father
and did only what the Father told Him to do. "So
Jesus explained, 'I tell you the truth, the Son can do
nothing by himself. He does only what he sees the
Father doing. Whatever the Father does, the Son also
does'" (John 5:19 NLT).

Jesus Has a Spiritual Fitness Plan

Have you ever wondered if Jesus had a specific plan or strategy for discipleship? Did He have a specific curriculum? If we had lived at that time, how would Jesus have discipled us? Does discipleship mean going to Bible study each week and spending time with other believers? Does discipleship occur when we finish reading a pile of classic Christian books?

If you were to walk into a fitness gym because you are out of shape, you would look for someone in great shape—someone you want to look like. Then you would ask what that person did to look that way. You would hope that person would reply, "If you do this workout, if you stay away from these types of food, and if you follow my plan with consistency, you will look like me." You would say, "Sign me up!" However, what if your fitness teacher said, "Why don't you get a gym membership, hang around this weight equipment, and just hope for the best?" You would say, "You've got to be kidding me!"

Is discipleship supposed to be a mystery—take some classes, read some books, and hope for the best? Or did Jesus have a specific plan so that He could confidently say, "You do this with consistency, and you will look like Me?" Jesus is your personal spiritual fitness trainer, and He told us exactly what He meant when He said to make disciples. He said, "Teach these new disciples to obey all the commands I have given you" (Matthew 28:20 NLT). Remember, at this point in His ministry, Jesus has just spent three years modeling a spirit-controlled life for His followers. They watched Him live every moment without once letting His circumstances rule Him. At the same time, they listened to Him for three years and heard Him explain everything to them in private. Jesus wants His disciples to teach new disciples to obey all that He commanded them, for "the very words I have spoken to you are spirit and life" (John 6:63 NLT).

> Is discipleship supposed to be a mystery—take some classes, read some books, and hope for the best? Or did Jesus have a specific plan so that He could confidently say, "You do this with consistency, and you will look like Me?"

Why is understanding Jesus' teaching about discipleship so important? Because we obeyed our flesh, our body, and our soul throughout our entire lives before we came to Christ. Your usual way of acting is to go with how you feel and think, and now that your spirit has come to life, you must learn to obey a new master. Your new master is righteousness (Romans 6:18).

> Your usual way of acting is to go with how you feel and think, and now that your spirit has come to life, you must learn to obey a new master. Your new master is righteousness (Romans 6:18).

The Blueprint for Spiritual Maturity

Perhaps you're thinking, "But I didn't personally get to see Jesus model the spirit-controlled life, and I didn't hear every single word He said in those three years that were 'spirit and life.'" However, God has given you a blueprint for discipleship. In His Word, He has laid out a plan for you to change the way you live. It isn't something new; it has been there all along. I call it the *Promise Principle* and I believe that Jesus taught it to His disciples.

In fact, if we could trust any group of people to know Jesus' form of discipleship, we would rely on His twelve close disciples. Out of those twelve, three spent a lot of one-on-one time with Him. Out of those three, Peter seemed to have a special relationship with Jesus. He became one of the most vocal teachers and writers about Jesus. Peter would have been an authority on

Jesus' plan for discipleship. Peter explains the plan; the *Promise Principle*:

> May God give you more and more grace and peace as you grow in your knowledge of God and Jesus our Lord.
>
> By his divine power, God has given us everything we need for living a godly life. We have received all of this by coming to know him, the one who called us to himself by means of his marvelous glory and excellence. And because of his glory and excellence, he has given us great and precious promises. These are the promises that enable you to share his divine nature and escape the world's corruption caused by human desires.
>
> In view of all this, make every effort to respond to God's promises (2 Peter 1:2–5a NLT)

This Scripture passage parallels the Great Commission, which calls us to go and make disciples, baptize them, and then teach them to obey. Peter says we are all made disciples by Christ's marvelous glory and excellence, which enables us to live a godly life. God has made it possible for us to obey Him because of His promises. A parallel version says it this way: "His divine power has given to us all things that *pertain* to life and godliness" (2 Peter 1:3 NKJV). Why is this verse true? Because life is still going to happen and circumstances will still arise, and God doesn't want us to obey our circumstances. He gave us everything we need to live a godly life. He promised that we could participate with and walk in His nature rather than our own. He has a method of discipling you to obey everything He has commanded. This plan includes responding to His promises.

A *principle* is a declared truth or a fundamental, primary law from which we derive other truths. In the *Promise Principle*, God declares that the fundamental way discipleship comes is through His promises, by which we participate in His nature rather than relying on our own nature. What are all of God's promises? *They are every truth and every commandment that He has revealed to us in His Word.* His promises are every truth that sets us free (John 8:38) and every commandment that is "spirit and life" (John 6:63 NLT). God's promises in Scripture are the will of the Spirit. If the Bible is God-breathed and its authors wrote every word through the illumination of the Spirit, then every promise in Scripture tells us how to be Spirit-led. It is through His promises that "we live and move and have our being" (Acts 17:28 ESV).

> In the *Promise Principle*, God declares that the fundamental way discipleship comes is through His promises, by which we participate in His nature rather than relying on our own nature.

For the word of God is alive and powerful. It is sharper than the sharpest two-edged sword, cutting between soul and spirit, between joint and marrow. It exposes our innermost thoughts and desires (Hebrews 4:12 NLT).

God's promises are His fundamental method to mature your spirit so that it can lead your soul. The author of Hebrews says that the Word of God is a double-edged sword that can cut between soul and spirit. God's Word can actually expose your most secret thoughts and desires. (Hebrews 4:12). If you respond to God's promises, you will be able to separate your spirit from these thoughts and desires so God's indwelling Spirit can lead you, rather than having your soul lead you. This process will allow your thoughts to be renewed. This isn't something that just happens merely because you are now a follower of Christ and your spirit is now alive. The Bible repeatedly says you must actively grow in this discipline. Paul says, "Since you have heard about Jesus and have learned the truth that comes from him, throw off your old sinful nature .... Instead, let the Spirit renew your thoughts and attitudes" (Ephesians 4:21–23 NLT).

Spiritual Creatine

In view of all this, make every effort to respond to God's promises. Supplement your faith with a generous provision of moral excellence, and moral excellence with knowledge, and knowledge with self-control, and self-control with patient endurance, and patient endurance with godliness, and godliness with brotherly affection, and brotherly affection with love for everyone (2 Peter 1:5–7 NLT)

When I was in college, I started working out in the same weight room with football players. There were some very big guys in there. As I came to know them, they started telling me that I needed a nutritional supplement. They said, "Phillip, you need to get on creatine." I didn't know what that was, so I remember thinking, "Are they telling me to take steroids?" Then a friend explained that creatine is simply an organic acid that occurs naturally in the human body and supplies energy to all its cells, primarily to muscle. Creatine powder is a supplement or additive that could enhance the work I was already doing to get bigger in the weight room. So I started taking creatine, and it did what it was supposed to do—it multiplied my efforts.

Peter says that if you respond to God's promises, you will supplement your faith with a generous provision of moral excellence, knowledge, self-control, patient endurance, godliness, and brotherly love. Why do you need a supplement of moral excellence? Because even as a believer, you will be tempted to make decisions that you will see as good at that moment—but they won't be morally excellent. Why do you need a supplement of brotherly affection? You need it because other people will sometimes betray and deeply wound you.

Spiritual Growth Takes Hard Work

The more you grow like this, the more productive and useful you will be in your knowledge of our Lord Jesus Christ. But those who fail to develop in this way are short-sighted or blind, forgetting that they have been cleansed from their old sins.

So, dear brothers and sisters, work hard to prove that you really are among those God has called and chosen. Do these things, and you will never fall away. Then God will give you a grand entrance into the eternal Kingdom of our Lord and Savior Jesus Christ (2 Peter 1:8–11 NLT).

The apostle Peter says God has given you a specific way to grow that will make you productive and useful in your knowledge of the Lord Jesus Christ, which means you can grow in knowledge but not be productive and useful. Many Christians have a lot of Bible knowledge. They can argue various kinds of theology and will willingly split their church to hold onto certain dogmas. Yet they don't possess any power or show any fruit in their lives. James says that they are merely hearers of God's Word and that they are deceived (James 1:22). A person can have great knowledge of God, yet live as deceived as someone God never saved and cleansed from sin. However, if you respond to the promises of God you will be productive. And I believe you want to be fruitful and productive.

Peter says you must work hard at this growth. Just as getting in shape physically requires hard work but promises results, so spiritual growth requires hard work but also promises results. Paul describes his spiritual training as more than just doing something and hoping for the best. Paul says we must train as intensely and purposefully as athletes:

> All athletes are disciplined in their training. They do it to win a prize that will fade away, but we do it for an eternal prize. So I run with purpose in every step. I am not just shadowboxing. I discipline my body like an athlete, training it to do what it should. Otherwise, I fear that after preaching to others I myself might be disqualified (1 Corinthians 9:25–27 NLT).

The Grand Entrance

The whole reason that an athlete trains for physical fitness is to win a prize that will fade away. But the reason that you train for spiritual fitness is to win an eternal prize. The apostle Peter says, "Then God will give you a grand entrance into the eternal Kingdom of our Lord and Savior Jesus Christ" (2 Peter 1:11 NLT). I want that grand entrance into the eternal kingdom where I get to stand before my Lord Jesus Christ.

Have you ever seen *Star Wars: A New Hope,* the first movie made in the series? It was the biggest movie of my childhood, and it has increased in popularity over the years. The last scene shows Princess Leia standing on a platform in a grand hall. All of the rebels (the good guys) are standing in this vast room in uniform and organized by their platoons. The music begins, and Luke Skywalker, Han Solo, and Chewbacca, who have just saved the day and destroyed the Death Star, make a grand entrance. Everyone turns at the exact same time at "attention." The music builds as they walk down the aisle and the crowd publicly honors them for their accomplishments. That scene is one of my favorite endings of any movie.[1]

Imagine all of heaven standing at attention as you make a grand entrance. The music builds as you walk down the center aisle. You move toward the King of Kings and Lord of Lords—the One who died for you, rescued you from certain eternal death, and gave you peace and a life full of meaningful relationships. You kneel to Him. King Jesus comes up to you and says (to paraphrase the NLT version of Matthew 25:23), "Well done, my good and faithful servant. You have been faithful in handling the small thing I have given you—a life of

---

1. George Lucas, *Star Wars: A New Hope* (Los Angeles: 20th Century Fox, 1977), Film.

80 years—so now I will give you many more responsibilities. Let's celebrate together!"

If Jesus says that to me, it will mean I have lived in obedience to His Word. It will mean I was a husband who laid my life down for my wife to present her as holy and blameless; I was a godly daddy who modeled love and obedience to the Lord and pointed my children in that direction. It will mean whatever area of influence I had in this life, I made an impact for the kingdom of God.

Do you feel like your efforts at discipleship are often like shadowboxing? You do the best you know to do, but you still feel spiritually weak. Do the circumstances of life seem to rule you? Do you feel that troubles cause you to blow like a leaf in the wind when it comes to your faith? Do you feel like you continually fall into the same temptations? God's Word contains all the promises that you need, and He has given them to you so you won't live by those circumstances in your life anymore. Learn how the *Promise Principle* works for your good.

> God's Word contains all the promises that you need, and He has given them to you so you won't live by those circumstances in your life anymore.

4

Throwing Mountains

British evangelist Smith Wigglesworth said something that I have always loved: "I am not moved by what I see. I am not moved by what I feel. I am moved only by what I believe."[1] The apostle Paul says, "For we live by believing and not by seeing" (2 Corinthians 5:7 NLT). As a disciple of Christ, you now live by faith and not by sight. Living by sight means that you act according to what you are experiencing right here and right now. You see circumstances and how they affect you. All of those things are right in front of you. You receive bad news from the doctor. You hear heart-wrenching words that your spouse doesn't love you any-more. Your son or daughter makes destructive decisions. Your good friend no longer acts like your friend because of hurt or unmet expectations. You experience and see things that create anxiety.

---

1. Allan G. Hedberg, *Lessons from My Father: 77 Mini Life Lessons from Dear Old Dad and Historical Fathers* (Nashville: Crossbooks, 2012), chap. 5.

George Müller, a famous German evangelist who lived in the eighteenth century, said, "The beginning of anxiety is the end of faith, and the beginning of true faith is the end of anxiety."[2] If you live by sight or according to your circumstances, anxiety fills you. If it consumes you, then it forces faith to leave. Yet if you are walking in faith, you are empty of all anxiety.

So what is faith? Is it just something you sing about? Is it just a religious word that we like to use? No. Faith is acting on the promises of God; in other words, it is responding to the promises of God. So how do you do that? Paul says, "Be anxious for nothing, but in everything by prayer and supplication, with thanksgiving, let your requests be made known to God" (Philippians 4:6 NKJV). God wants you to respond by praying about everything. Every trouble and every temptation—you can actually talk to Him about it and respond to Him in every circumstance. As you deal with "everything by prayer," you can respond to God's promises in two ways: with supplication and with thanksgiving. You can ask by faith (supplication), and you can receive with thanksgiving. Sometimes it is one or the other, and sometimes it is both. Look at the first of these two ways you can respond.

---

2. John Ortberg, Kevin Harney, and Sherry Harney, *Stepping out in Faith: Life-changing Examples from the History of Israel* (Grand Rapids, MI: Zondervan, 2003).

> As you deal with "everything by prayer," you can respond to God's promises in two ways: with supplication and with thanksgiving. You can ask by faith (supplication), and you can receive with thanksgiving. Sometimes it is one or the other, and sometimes it is both.

Asking by Faith

> And whatever things you ask in prayer, believing, you will receive (Matthew 21:22 NKJV).

You might think I will teach you a "name it and claim it" strategy. However, this lesson has nothing to do with using the "power of faith" to create your own reality or simply get what you want. Paul tells us to pray about everything; we are to ask God in faith, and we are to receive with thanksgiving. He doesn't say we will get anything we want if we pray in this way (Philippians 4:6–7).

Paul declares, "Then you will experience God's peace, which exceeds anything we can understand. His peace will guard your hearts and minds as you live in Christ Jesus" (Philippians 4:7 NLT). If you will pray about everything, no matter what the circumstances,

He will give you peace (wholeness) and guard your heart and mind. He will guard your feelings and thoughts. God is more interested in changing you than in changing your circumstances. In fact, He does this to help you mature spiritually, as I said earlier. God brings you to a place where you can say that, although everything isn't well with your circumstances, it is well with your soul. Why can you say it is well with your soul? When you receive God's promises you can have real wholeness in Christ, even if you are walking through hard things.

A Withered Tree

Now in the morning, as He returned to the city, He was hungry. And seeing a fig tree by the road, He came to it and found nothing on it but leaves, and said to it, "Let no fruit grow on you ever again." Immediately the fig tree withered away.

And when the disciples saw it, they marveled, saying, "How did the fig tree wither away so soon?"

So Jesus answered and said to them, "Assuredly, I say to you, if you have faith and do not doubt, you will not only do what was done to the fig tree, but also if you say to this mountain, 'Be removed and be cast into the sea,' it will be done. And whatever things you ask in prayer, believing, you will receive" (Matthew 21:18–22 NKJV).

This story precedes Jesus' instructions to His disciples in which He taught them that if they would ask for anything in prayer, believing, they would receive it. In this story, Jesus curses an actual fig tree, and it withers in front of the disciples. He tells them they can do things like this. However, I also want you to realize that the fig tree represents Israel. The Israelites were the fig tree that wasn't bearing fruit. It represented the spiritual deadness of God's people. Jesus saw it and cursed it. The tree had leaves, and from a distance it looked like it should have had fruit. Christians can have that same kind of experience. We can look good from far away, but when you get closer and examine our lives, we are fruitless and unproductive.

Then Jesus tells the disciples that if they have faith, they can even uproot a mountain and throw it into the sea. Jesus instructs us about the way God will give us whatever we need to walk in spiritual fruitfulness, rather than getting what we want for our flesh. Mountains can represent any obstacle in your life; any temptation or any circumstance that keeps you from walking by the Spirit. What are the mountains in your life that you would like to throw into the sea?

Mountains can represent any obstacle in your life; any temptation or any circumstance that keeps you from walking by the Spirit.

My Personal Mountain

I also have had to throw many mountains, or circumstances, into the sea. One of the big mountains in my life has been hurt and unforgiveness toward people from the church. When I was 16, I believed the Lord had called me into full-time ministry. I thought that God had called me to become a pastor because my dad was a pastor. I had been involved in some form of ministry my entire life. But when I was a senior in high school, the church fired my dad. The conflict concerned spiritual authority and church people not wanting to follow it. Some church members spread all kinds of lies and slandered our family to the community.

When this happened, I really struggled with forgiveness. How could church people who said they love God do such a thing? I made an inner vow that I would never work for a church. I didn't want my wife and children to know the hurt and ugliness I experienced. It took many years to walk through that healing.

After twenty years of doing ministry outside of the church, I finally joined the staff of a church. In the first month, some individuals complained that they didn't like some things I believed about certain passages of Scripture, so they made false statements about me. They sent emails filled with accusations and half-truths. I lost several friendships and ended up leaving a church that I had been a member of as a young person. This situation hurt because I loved the people, and they believed I had let them down. The "mountains" of slander about my family from people whom I once considered close friends felt more like a mountain range than a single mountain.

I watched my parents repeat this kind of experience with their church. As their son, my soul wanted to indulge in evil desires such as bitterness, resentment, and hatred. In fact, there have been times when I mentally rehearsed all the things I wanted to say to those people. My sinful nature wants to respond to what I feel and think. On the other hand, because I have faith in God's promises, I want to respond to the Holy Spirit. So as I walk through those circumstances—I must act on the promises of God.

I mentioned earlier that God's Word contains two types of promises: *truths and commandments*. I have learned that every commandment is a promise from God that will bring me life. The problem is I don't have the ability to follow any commandment in my own strength. The Bible says we can't even say that Jesus Christ is Lord without the power of the Holy Spirit (1 Corinthians 12:3). If I can't even say, "Jesus is Lord" without the Holy Spirit, then there is no command in Scripture that I can follow without the Spirit's power. This is why Jesus says to ask in faith.

> I have learned that every commandment is a promise from God that will bring me life. The problem is I don't have the ability to follow any commandment in my own strength.

Here is one of those commandments: "Instead, clothe yourself with the presence of the Lord Jesus Christ. And don't let yourself think about ways to indulge your evil desires" (Romans 13:14 NLT). This particular promise tells me not to indulge in any evil desire, but rather to be clothed in God's presence. What I have had to do many times in my situation is respond to this promise. The way I respond is by doing everything by prayer (Philippians 4:6). So, I pray:

Lord Jesus, I love You and need You. My heart is hurt- ing, and I am in anguish. My soul desires to fill itself with bitterness and hurt. I want to indulge this feeling and feed it, but I ask You to strengthen me by Your Spirit (Ephesians 3:16) and clothe me with Your presence. I want to be clothed with compassion, kindness, and patience (Colossians 3:12). I humble myself before You (James 4:6), and my eyes are fixed on You (Hebrews 12:2). Now I receive Your peace. Thank You for guarding my heart and my mind (Philippians 4:7). In Jesus' name, Amen.

Did you notice all the promises I prayed from Scripture? Later in the book, you will learn how you can do this. I actually said this prayer a few days ago while driving to work. As I prayed and responded to the promise of clothing myself with His presence by asking for it, the Lord filled my heart with peace. He then told me to do something my soul would never have wanted to do. He said, "Appreciate them." I didn't argue; I began to thank God for these people, many of whom were once close friends. My heart was immediately able to thank God for all the sweet times I had with them. I was able to thank Him for all the times they had been a blessing. Then God gave me the perspective that Jesus had: "Father, forgive them, for they don't know what they are doing" (Luke 23:34 NLT). In their hurt and unmet expectations, the people who hurt me were only acting out of what they felt and thought. And in that moment, my faith was able to throw that mountain into the sea.

A Hurting Son

I have not stopped thanking God for you. I pray for you constantly, asking God, the glorious Father of our Lord Jesus Christ, to give you spiritual wisdom and insight so that you might grow in your knowledge of God. I pray that your hearts will be flooded with light so that you can understand the confident hope he has given to those he called—his holy people who are his rich and glorious inheritance (Ephesians 1:16–18 NLT).

At Gateway Church, we launched *Promise Principle* for our discipleship groups. In Chapter 9, I will show you how these groups operate, but for now, I will give you another example of "asking in faith" and throwing a mountain into the sea. In one group, we were going through the book of Ephesians and underlining all of God's promises. A man underlined verses 17 and 18 in chapter 1 and said, "I figure if the Holy Spirit put on the apostle Paul's heart to ask for spiritual wisdom and insight into the knowledge of God, then maybe it is something I could ask for as well." I asked him about a circumstance that was robbing him of peace so that he needed spiritual wisdom. In tears, he told our group that his son had just attempted suicide the day before, and he and his wife didn't know how to react as parents. He told us how the circumstances tore their hearts and how they needed God's wisdom.

I reminded him that we bring "everything in prayer"; I suggested that he take this supplication to the Lord and respond to God's promise. The man bowed his head and prayed:

> Heavenly Father, I come before You and lift up my son to You. I thank You that You have given him to us. I ask You, Lord, to fill my wife and me with spiritual wisdom and insight about Your perfect knowledge for this situation. Would You give us direction and lead us? I also pray that You would fill our son's heart with light, no matter what darkness is filling him right now, that he would understand the confident hope that he has in You. We trust You, Lord! Amen.

The man looked up, wiped the tears from his eyes, and smiled at the rest of the group. His circumstance hadn't changed, but God was filling his heart with peace.

As parents, because we love our children, their troubles can also be huge mountains for us to conquer. Throw them into the sea! God is in control. This dad was throwing his mountain into the sea and he knew it in his spirit. The rest of the story is that when his son came home from the hospital, this dad started teaching him how to pray and respond to the promises of God.

Lord, Be with Us

You just read Ephesians 1:16 a few minutes ago. Paul wrote, "I have not stopped thanking God for you. I pray for you constantly, asking God...." There are two things he is doing. He thanks God for his readers and he petitions God for them. We have two ways we respond to God. We ask in faith and we receive with thanksgiving. Most believers don't know how to respond to their circumstances. They don't take all things to the Lord in prayer. And when they pray, all they know to do is ask God to help someone. Most of the prayers we hear in church sound like this: "Lord, we just ask that You would be with us today. And we ask that You would be with brother Bob as he is in the hospital. We pray that You would be with Sally as she is taking her test. And be with us as we go our separate ways. Amen."

Do your prayers sound like the ones above? Is "the Lord's presence" a truth from God's Word that you need to ask Him for or one that you should receive with thanksgiving?

> So be strong and courageous! Do not be afraid and do not panic before them. For the Lord your God will personally go ahead of you. He will neither fail you nor abandon you. Do not be afraid or discouraged, for the Lord will personally go ahead of you. He will be with you; he will neither fail you nor abandon you (Deuteronomy 31:6, 8 NLT)

This is my command—be strong and courageous! Do not be afraid or discouraged. For the Lord your God is with you wherever you go (Joshua 1:9 NLT).

Don't be afraid, for I am with you.
> Don't be discouraged, for I am your God.
I will strengthen you and help you.
> I will hold you up with my victorious right hand.
"See, all your angry enemies lie there,
> confused and humiliated.
Anyone who opposes you will die
> and come to nothing.
You will look in vain
> for those who tried to conquer you.
Those who attack you
> will come to nothing.
For I hold you by your right hand—
> I, the Lord your God.
And I say to you,
> 'Don't be afraid. I am here to help you'"
(Isaiah 41:10 13 NLT).

"I will never fail you.
I will never abandon you."
So we can say with confidence,
"The Lord is my helper,
> so I will have no fear.
> What can mere people do to me?" (Hebrews 13:5–6 NLT).

Please don't skip over these verses—they will encourage you. God's Word promises over and over again that He is with us wherever we go. In fact, He is emphatic about it. These are only a few of the multitude of verses that promise God is with us. He is serious about the promise that He is with us no matter where we go. In fact, go back and underline every time God says He is with you or He will not abandon you.

> God's Word promises over and over again that He is with us wherever we go. In fact, He is emphatic about it.

We let our feelings and circumstances rule our hearts when we feel as though we are alone. Don't live by sight during these times—walk in faith. Act on the promise of God and thank Him for His presence saying,

Heavenly Father, I praise You that You are omnipresent. I receive this truth, and I am so thankful for Your presence. I thank You that You will not abandon me. I thank You because You are here to help me. I thank You because even if I am having the worst day possible, Your Word says that even if my soul feels like it is in the pit of Hell (Psalm 139:8), You are there. Holy Spirit, I ask you to make me aware of Your presence. Amen.

I hope you never ask God to "be with you" again. Receive His truth and walk in it. This belief is important in your journey of growing in spiritual maturity. If you are continually asking God for something He is already doing, it is as if you are not taking Him at His word. You might go so far as to say that isn't a prayer of faith. You might think I am belaboring this point—because I am. Did you notice how I ended the prayer above? "Holy Spirit, I ask you to make me aware of your presence." This request is different from asking God to do something He has already promised. Instead, this is saying, "God, I know You are with me, but my circumstances right now are overwhelming me and I need Your help."

When you pray for your child, don't say, "Lord, would You be with my son today as he is at school?" You know He is with your child according to His Word. So the way you should respond to the promise is by praying, "Lord, I thank You that You are with my son when he is at school. I trust You and thank You for Your protection over his life. I ask that You would make him aware of Your presence, that he wouldn't feel alone, and that in all of his decisions he will know You are there."

I am not just playing word games. A shift happens when you pray according to the promises of God. Jesus said, "If you remain in me, and my words remain in you, ask whatever you wish, and it will be done for you" (John 15:7 NIV). If you are bringing all things to Him in prayer and if His promises are what you respond to, Jesus is promising that what you ask will be done. But asking in faith is more about spiritual fruitfulness than about getting what you want. God's Word contains many commandments and life-giving promises. I can't live them out in my own strength. God's Word tells me to forgive because Christ first forgave me (Colossians 3:13), to walk in humility (Micah 6:8), to think on things that are pure (Philippians 4:8), to not to grow weary in doing good (Galatians 6:9), and so many other commands that promise to bring me life.

> Asking in faith is more about spiritual fruitfulness than about getting what you want.

As I act on God's promises, I can live out these things by asking in faith for the Holy Spirit to enable me. Paul knew this when he wrote, "I pray that from his glorious, unlimited resources he will empower you with inner strength through his Spirit" (Ephesians 3:16 NLT). You can throw mountains because God will use His unlimited resources to empower you with strength. In Christ, you can throw any mountain into the sea!

5

Receive the Gizzard

And give thanks for everything to God the Father in the name of our Lord Jesus Christ (Ephesians 5:20 NLT).

Parenthood teaches many things about life—truths I am learning as I teach our children. As our children grow, one of our deepest desires is for them to have grateful hearts. They have been given so much that it is easy for them to "take a gift" for their birthday or for Christmas. I say they "take a gift" because to "receive" means accepting it for all it is intended to be. Often they just open it and move on to the next present. As parents, we have to remind our kids to say, "Thank you" to the giver. If we give them something and they express gratitude, we experience a blessing as parents, but the receiver can experience a blessing through this principle as well.

This past year, we took our children to Disney World. If you have ever gone, you know it isn't cheap, and it has nothing to do with rest and relaxation. We take our children because we want them to experience the magic and adventure. Parents sacrifice because we love our children, and so we express that love through blessing them. So why is it so frustrating when they have emotional meltdowns? Why does it hurt our hearts when they complain or want more?

We experience blessing as parents when our children receive with thanksgiving. We want our children to be able to see the time that went into the gift, or the sacrifice that the giver made. If they could more fully understand the preciousness of the gift, they could better receive it with a grateful heart. The result is a fuller blessing for them and for the giver as well.

The Blessing of Receiving

> Whatever is good and perfect is a gift coming down to us from God our Father (James 1:17 NLT).

One afternoon while visiting Tanzania, a local pastor invited me to dinner in his home. The walls and roof of the house consisted of tin and cardboard. The floor was dirt. My seat was an upside-down milk crate. I was the guest of honor. With pride, they brought to the table a huge mound of rice, beans, and a whole chicken that I had seen running around the front of the home just a few hours earlier. The hosts served every major organ of the bird, including the gizzard. I remember thinking, "This isn't how the chicken looks at my local chicken restaurant." They served my plate, and my portion included the gizzard.

I confess I really struggled with a strong gag reflex when I was younger. If I thought something didn't taste good, because of my predisposition, it would cause me to gag. My parents called it "pickiness," but I chose a more positive term for my condition: "being particular." I was only being particular about what I put in my body.

Before I made a disgusted face about the gizzard or said something I would later regret, my translator leaned over and said, "They believe the gizzard is a delicacy, and it is reserved for the guest of honor. They want you to have it at this meal." Because of my love for the people and my desire not to be rude, my attitude about the gizzard changed. Not only was I going to *take* the gizzard, I was going to *receive* it with gratefulness. If you can understand the sacrifice, you can receive with a thankful heart. You can even receive a gizzard with thanks. You can't truly receive anything from anyone without gratefulness. If you don't have gratefulness, you are just taking—not receiving.

> You can't truly receive anything from anyone without gratefulness. If you don't have gratefulness, you are just taking—not receiving.

God's Word contains many different truths. These promises of God are truths you must receive. If you won't receive them, you don't get them. If you can't receive them with a heart full of gratitude, you really won't get the fullness of the truth. For example, God offers you forgiveness. John says, "He is faithful and just to forgive us our sins" (1 John 1:9 NLT). Paul says, "*There is* therefore now no condemnation to those who are in Christ Jesus" (Romans 8:1 NKJV). One of my favorite promises reads, "Even if we feel guilty, God is greater than our feelings, and he knows everything" (1 John 3:20 NLT). Just because God offers forgiveness to you in heaven doesn't mean you live in and experience forgiveness here on earth—unless you are willing to receive it.

God's Word offers these truths. Can you receive them with a heart full of gratitude? Many of us have acquired so much truth in our lives through sermons or books that we merely "take truth." I know that when I take truth, I only hear it, but I don't receive it. God wants us to receive truth with gratitude. If you receive it, then that truth will set you free. Any truth in God's Word that you can't receive with thanksgiving is a truth that will not set you free. Freedom comes when you can receive the truth with a full heart of gratitude.

> Any truth in God's Word that you can't receive with thanksgiving is a truth that will not set you free. Freedom comes when you can receive the truth with a full heart of gratitude.

It also blesses the Father when we receive with thanksgiving. Receiving promises from God is a part of our faith. The author of Hebrews says, "It is impossible to please God without faith" (Hebrews 11:6 NLT). It pleases the Father when His children trust Him. God's Word teaches that Jesus died on the cross so that God might save us. Do you "take Jesus" and merely add Him to your life, or do you "receive Jesus" with a heart full of gratitude to be everything He can be in your life? We have only one way that we can please the Father. Many people have taken Jesus and only added Him to their lives. If you haven't received Jesus, receive Him now.

Arguing God's Promises

Just as He chose us in Him before the foundation of the world, that we should be holy and without blame before Him in love, having predestined us to adoption as sons by

Jesus Christ to Himself, according to the good pleasure of His will, to the praise of the glory of His grace, by which He made us accepted in the Beloved (Ephesians 1:4–6 NKVJ)

I was training some leaders at one of Gateway Church's campuses on how to lead a *Promise Principle* group when we came to this passage in Ephesians—a passage that, in most Christian circles, leads believers to argue about their ideas of predestination and free will. In those situations, everyone wants to know who is an Arminian and who is a Calvinist. However, will that help people learn to obey everything that Jesus spoke? Will this debate give life and help us follow the Spirit?

The enemy plots to instigate God's people to argue about God's promises. As a parent, I don't want my children to argue about the things that I tell them. I simply want them to respond in obedience. Do we miss receiving the power of God's promises because we spend too much time fighting over our opinion of the truth?

One of our *Promise Principle* leaders had underlined Ephesians 1:4–5. So I asked him if he thought that particular passage was something he needed to ask God for or was it something he needed to receive with thanksgiving. He told me it was something he needed to thank God for since God had already done it. Then I asked him what circumstance was keeping him from being liberated by this promise. The man began to share how he often felt that God couldn't really forgive him. If everyone knew about his past, he would be disqualified as a leader. I told him another truth from God's Word: The accuser attacks us day and night, and God promises that we can overcome him by the blood of the Lamb and the word of our testimony (Revelation 12:10–11). Therefore, we have the blood of Jesus and the Word of God to stand against those lies of the enemy.

> Do we miss receiving the power of God's promises because we spend too much time fighting over our opinion of the truth?

I asked this leader whose voice he thought he was hearing when he believed that lie. He knew the accuser was responsible for that deception. "What is the Holy Spirit saying to you right now?" I asked. Immediately, he responded, "God chose me as His son, He adopted me, and He was pleased to do it." I told him to pray that promise—"everything in prayer," bring your request to God. The leader began to pray,

Dear Father ... Daddy, even though I feel like You could never forgive me of my sin, or that You could never love me because of my past, I thank You that You chose me. You adopted me as Your son, and it was Your will and great pleasure to do it. I don't deserve Your love, but I receive it right now. In Jesus' name I pray, Amen.

As that man prayed, tears began to flow because those promises weren't just information in his head anymore. When we say something aloud, we are laying the foundation for an idea in our head. One of the most important things that we can do is to allow the Holy Spirit to move information from our head into our heart and soul. Then it becomes transformational, and the Holy Spirit can renew our thoughts and attitudes in those areas (Ephesians 4:23).

From Your Head to Your Heart

How do our thoughts and attitudes change? "Do everything in prayer." God is Spirit, and He gave you a spirit to relate to Him. Prayer engages your spirit. When that group leader told us aloud about his circumstances and the truth he knew from God's Word, he was processing all those things in his head. But when he began to pray that truth and receive it, his spirit engaged, and God began to minister and speak to him about that truth. Someone has said that the furthest distance is between the head and the heart. It is only a long distance if we don't know how to take truths from our heads to our hearts. The shortest route is "receiving it through prayer."

When you start "receiving it through prayer," God begins the process of hiding His Word in your heart so that you won't sin against Him (Psalm 119:11). The word the psalmist used for "heart" means the center of your feelings or your soul. As you pray and respond to God's Word with your spirit, He hides His truth in the center of your emotional soul. We hide His Word in our feelings because God uses this means to renew our thoughts and attitudes. George Whitfield, an important leader of the Great Awakening in the eighteenth century, wrote, "I began to read the Holy Scriptures upon my knees, laying aside all other books, and praying over, if possible, every line and word. This proved meat indeed and drink indeed to my soul. I daily received fresh life, light, and power from above."[1] This is how God renews our hearts and minds.

Has the Holy Spirit ever changed your heart? I served as a student pastor for about 15 years. Almost 10 years ago, I met Maggie, a high school freshman. She grew up in a home filled with abuse and neglect. This experience took an enormous toll on Maggie's self-worth. I received many phone calls in the middle of the night because her

1. L. Tyerman, *The Life of the Rev. George Whitefield* (New York: Anson D.F. Randolph, 1877), 36.

mom locked her out of the house with nowhere else for her to go. Maggie struggled with depression and suicidal thoughts. Despite her past, the Holy Spirit began renewing Maggie's thoughts and feelings about herself. As she responded to God's promises and received them with thanksgiving in her heart, God took His Word and hid it in the feelings of her heart. Low self-esteem and depression no longer rule this area of her life. As Maggie began to change, her mother took notice. Maggie's mom died from cancer, but before that happened her mom came to the Lord. She told me that Maggie was her hero. Maggie is now on staff and leading teenage girls in the same student ministry where she first met Jesus.

The process of renewing our thoughts and attitudes doesn't happen simply by years of church attendance. I have counseled many people who have attended church since birth, but still struggle with their identity and feelings of low self-worth. These feelings affect their relationships and responses to every circumstance. Only when we allow God to hide His truth in the center of our feelings does He renew our thoughts and attitudes.

> Only when we allow God to hide His truth in the center of our feelings does He renew our thoughts and attitudes.

Don't Reject It

> Since everything God created is good, we should not reject
> any of it but receive it with thanks (1 Timothy 4:4 NLT).

How incredible is it that we can "take" truth but not
"receive" it? Earlier I wrote about the way my children often "take" gifts rather than "receive" them. We
all share the propensity to take and not receive. When
we "take" advice or "take" a compliment, it's as if we
are really rejecting it. Pride resides in our heart, so we
refuse to receive. It takes humility to "receive" advice or
a compliment.

How good are you at receiving advice? One of the
phrases I have used with my father, even as an adult was,
"I know!" He would give me some advice and I would
respond, "I know!" One day the Lord convicted me and
I realized that every time I said, "I know" to someone,
pride was residing in my heart. I struggled to receive
advice whether I needed it or not. The truth is I need all
the advice I can get.

Do you also struggle with receiving compliments?
When you have done something good or someone tries to
affirm you, do you have difficulty receiving it? If you are
truly honest with yourself, your spirit actually rejoices
in the compliment, but pride causes you to struggle
with receiving it, so you just "take" it. Most of us have

difficulty in this area. Sometimes we deflect the compliment by saying something like, "Oh, it's no big deal," or we return the compliment back to the person who gave it in a way that diminishes its value.

As children, we had a saying: "I'm rubber, you're glue—whatever you say bounces off me and sticks to you." We would use it when someone said something mean to us. However, we sometimes act that way with affirming words. We take the compliments, but we throw them right back at the giver. Of course you should encourage other people, but can you receive a compliment? Maybe the Lord is using that person to affirm you, but you can't receive the Father's love because of pride. God doesn't want us to reject anything He has made. He is the one who has created all truth, so we should receive all of it. We must have a shift in our attitude for this to happen.

I Receive It

My wife and I have learned to speak affirming words of life over our children before they go to bed. It doesn't happen every night, but we try to make a habit of it. When we come to their bed, my wife and I take turns telling them we love them. We tell them how proud we are of them and share something good that we see in them. We call out gifts and talents in their lives. We have a rule that they can't reply with "Thank you, Daddy" or "I love you, too, Mommy"—they can only reply, "I receive it." It is incredible to watch their faces and eyes when they simply receive it.

I have also begun to say, "I receive it" in the middle of worship songs as I am singing. If the song is about God's faithfulness, I tell the Lord that I receive it regardless of my circumstances. I know this doesn't rhyme with the lyrics, but the power of the truth that I am singing goes so much deeper when I tell the Lord, "I receive it!"

I once was in Ohio speaking at a retreat with a church as they launched new *Promise Principle* groups. One man confessed to me that he felt he was a bad father and he had been verbally abusive to his children. He wanted to repent and confess his sin to God. I prayed with this man, and then told him the Father wanted him to know he was forgiven. I asked the man if he could receive it. He told me it was very hard and he didn't really think he could. Then I told him again, "The Father says, 'I forgive you.'" Then I asked him again if he could receive it. The man told me he just didn't feel like he could.

I responded by asking him what was his authority. He looked at me puzzled. I explained that his authority could either be God's Word or his thoughts and feelings. Which one would he choose? Immediately, he responded, "The Word of God is my authority!" Then I told him that if God's Word was his authority, he would have to receive it—he couldn't base his life on what he felt or thought. Right then, he said, "I receive it!" The moment he said those words the shame broke. Tears began to flow down his cheeks.

The Holy Spirit then led me to say, "Your Heavenly Father loves you and is so proud of you." After I said these words, I asked him if he also could receive them. He didn't respond, so I simply asked again, "What is your authority?" He responded, "God's Word and His promises." I said, "Okay, then what do you say about God being proud of you and calling you 'son'"? He replied, "I receive it." Even though this man had confessed his sin and God had forgiven him, he didn't yet walk in the forgiveness and cleansing that 1 John 1:9 talks about until he received it.

What is your authority? What is the truth that you need to receive with thanksgiving? The psalmist tells you that you are "fearfully and wonderfully made" (Psalm 139:14 NKJV). Can you say, "I receive it"? "He cares for you" (1 Peter 5:7 NKJV). Can you say, "I receive it"? "Even if we feel guilty, God is greater than our feelings, and he knows everything" (1 John 3:20 NLT). Can you say, "I receive it"? The Bible says that Jesus died on the cross to pay for all your sins. You can do nothing to earn His salvation. John says, "But to all who did receive him, who believed in his name, he gave the right to become children of God" (John 1:12 ESV). Can you say, "I receive it"? Even though all the promises of God belong to you, you won't experience them if you can't receive them. Any truth you can't receive is a truth that won't set you free.

> Even though all the promises of God belong to you, you won't experience them if you can't receive them. Any truth you can't receive is a truth that won't set you free.

6

Why the Bible? — Part 1

I am neither a psychologist nor a practicing counselor. I am a pastor who has ministered to people through their heartaches and struggles. When people share their thoughts and feelings with me, I pray the entire time. I say, "Holy Spirit, I need You to speak to me right now so I will have a word or spiritual wisdom that is from You to give them." All the things I share here God has taught me from years of talking with people.

Nearly every time I encounter struggling people, I find they have focused their eyes on their circumstances rather than the Lord. Much like the man from the Ohio church, they can't receive God's promises because they don't feel them in their hearts. Do you experience them? When you experience overwhelming, painful circumstances, how do you respond? Do the promises in God's Word make a difference? Do you struggle to forgive yourself or others? Do you encounter anxiety because you fear you will lack provision in the future? Do you ever feel worthless or unloved?

What is the authority for your life? Do you really believe God's Word is trustworthy? Or do you trust your feelings and thoughts? A change in authority must happen. When you became a follower of Jesus, He became your authority instead of you. His Word and His promises must become authoritative in your life if you are going to be transformed by the renewing of your mind (Romans 12:2).

Read again the Great Commission: "Therefore, go and make disciples of all the nations. ... Teach these new disciples to obey all the commands I have given you" (Matthew 28:19–20 NLT). We have to be taught to obey all His commands. In other words, we have to make all of His commands authoritative in our life. Another way to say the Great Commission is once you settle the issue of Jesus being the authority, you must conclude that everything He has spoken is also your authority.

For the Bible to become your authority, you have to ask if you believe the Bible is trustworthy. You may have grown up hearing that the Bible is true, but you never developed your own point of view. Imagine yourself as someone who is not yet a believer. If someone quoted Scripture to you, you might say to yourself, "Why should I care? The Bible has no weight or authority in my life." Or pretend that someone came up to you today and began quoting a principle from a book called *Tin-Buck-Two*. If he said, "According to *Tin-Buck-Two,* if you pray to Kabuna and believe in him, you will never die," would you receive that truth? You probably would not, because that book holds no authority in your life. This experience is similar to that of a non-believer who hears a Christian quote from the Bible.

I don't want to dismiss the fact that God's Word is alive and active, and the Holy Spirit can convict people even if the Bible isn't their authority. However, He usually does not work that way. Unless something is authoritative in your life, you won't obey it. Ask yourself this question: "Have I made a commitment in my heart to the authority of Scripture?"

Once you settle the issue of Jesus being the authority, you must conclude that everything He has spoken is also your authority.

What Is Good for You Is Good for Me

Do you like ice cream? What is your favorite flavor? It might be chocolate or vanilla—or maybe you like peppermint chocolate chip. If I said chocolate was the best flavor, and you said vanilla was the best, who would be right? Neither of us is right. Ice cream flavors are a matter of personal preference. But what if I asked you to tell me where the Nile River flows? You could immediately say, "Egypt" or "parts of Africa." But what if I disagree and say the Nile River is in Australia? Which one of us is right now? Can we both be right? No, because this is an issue of facts, not personal preference. If someone had taught me for my entire life that the Nile is in Australia, could I be wrong? The answer is "Yes."

It is possible to believe something that is untrue. Just because you believe with all your heart that the Nile River is in Australia doesn't mean that it suddenly starts to form there. I can believe something with all my heart; genuinely believe it—but be genuinely wrong. Truth is something discovered, not something created.

Many people consider opinions about faith, God, the Creation, the Bible, and world religions on a par with ice cream flavors. They consider beliefs about those things to be personal preferences or opinions. So they say, "What's good for you is good for you, and what's good for me is good for me." Our society considers people "tolerant" if they feel that way about faith. If you feel otherwise, you are "intolerant."

How has the definition of "truth" evolved in contemporary society? Consider these two different sets of definitions. Here is a contemporary definition of truth[1]:

---

1. https://en.oxforddictionaries.com/definition/truth (Accessed 13 October 2016).

1. The quality or state of being true.

2. That which is true or in accordance with fact or reality.

3. A fact or *belief that is accepted as true.*

Notice the shift in the definition over the last two hundred years from Noah Webster's Dictionary of 1828[2]:

1. Conformity to fact or reality.

2. Purity from falsehood.

3. **Exactness, the real state of things, absolute.**

Our society has changed truth from "a fact" or "an absolute" to a belief that is "accepted as true." That's a significant difference. A parent might say, "Tell me the truth, Johnny! Who broke the lamp?" Johnny's older sister walks in and says, "I believe it was the dog, Rascal." Yet the parent sees Johnny's face, so she asks again, "Johnny, who broke the lamp?" The parent doesn't want an opinion. He wants to know what happened.

> Our society has changed truth from "a fact" or "an absolute" to a belief that is "accepted as true."

2. *Noah Webster's 1828 American Dictionary of the English Language,* https://1828.mshaffer.com/d/word/truth (accessed 13 October 2016). Noah Webster compiled the first English dictionary and used the Bible as the basis for his definitions.

The truth is what actually happened. Opinion has nothing to do with it. When Creation occurred, there is the truth of what actually happened. Only one thing can be true. There is a truth about what actually happens when we die. It will not be a different reality for each person based on their personal preference or belief. We can't create our own truth. Truth is something we discover—somewhat like the Nile River. The problem is we don't really get to discover what will actually happen after death until we die, which may be too late.

Some people hold certain beliefs because of the way they grew up. Certain beliefs surrounded them in their culture. Others choose themselves as their own authority. Working from their experiences, they interpret everything through their perspectives. They make decisions and claim to evaluate the purpose of life and eternity from their own points of view. Your own opinion is a sketchy place from which to draw convictions about eternity when you possess such a finite understanding.

You might also ask, "What authority has the most evidence?" You don't want to be wrong, and if you are going to choose something, you want it to have the greatest reliability. God gave you a brain. When it comes to faith, God never asks you to have blind faith or to check reason at the door. He gave you the ability to think and consider. If we went skydiving at 14,000 feet and I opened the plane door and prepared to jump with no parachute, you would say, "Wait, don't jump!" If I replied, "I'm not worried; God will take care of me—my faith is in Him," you would think to yourself, "Well, that is the most insane thing I have ever heard." You would tell me to put my faith in the parachute because it is designed to protect me and bring me safely to the ground. God never promised that if I simply have blind faith, He would catch me after I jump out of a plane—I would jump, and I would die.

God doesn't ask us to have blind faith. He has gone to great lengths to provide us with so much revelation about who He is and what life is about. He gave us the Bible so that we might know Him. What internal and external evidence exists for the trustworthiness of the Bible?

The Bible Itself — Internal Evidence #1

The word Bible comes from the Greek word *Byblos*. Originally, the word denoted a small papyrus plant that was used as writing material. As large quantities of this papyrus were exported from Egypt to Phoenicia, the term "Byblos" began to be used as the name of the port city in what is today known as Lebanon.[3] As early as the third and second century BC, the Jewish Greeks were

---

3. David Ewert, *A General Introduction to the Bible* (Grand Rapids, MI: Zondervan, 1990), 20.

already using the term *biblia* (plural) for the scrolls containing the Jewish Holy Scriptures, which were kept in the synagogues.[4] This word was also used by first century Christians; for example, the apostle Paul used the term *biblia* in the Greek text when asking Timothy to bring his "books," or parchments (2 Timothy 4:13).

The authors of the Bible's individual books lived over the span of 1,500 years. They all couldn't have known each other, and they certainly didn't come together to get their stories "straight." Some were shepherds, some kings, some prophets, and one grew up in the house of Pharaoh. Some were fishermen, one was a physician, one was a tax collector, one was the actual brother of Jesus, and one even murdered Christians before Jesus changed his life. Yet all of their stories agree. The Bible is perfect. Even though there were almost 40 authors, the Holy Spirit guided them all. That is why the Bible contains no contradictions.

You might have just held your breath when you read that last sentence. Perhaps you have heard that the Bible contains contradictions. Don't let that accusation scare you. It doesn't scare me anymore. I have looked long and hard and traveled through Scripture many times. There are no contradictions. There are things that my mind can't grasp, but with God, there are no contradictions.

---

4. Michael D. Coogan, ed., *The Oxford Encyclopedia of the Books of the Bible* (Oxford: Oxford University Press, 2011), 1:75.

Someone once said to me, "But wait—one of the Ten Commandments says, 'Thou shalt not kill.' Yet the Bible has stories of God telling the Israelites to destroy the Amalekites. Isn't that a contradiction?" The word "kill" in the King James Version is more precisely translated as "murder" (the unlawful taking of a human life), as it is in the New King James and most modern translations. God allowed the Israelites under the Old Covenant to kill others for extraordinary reasons, such as punishment for murder (Exodus 21:12–14), adultery (Leviticus 20:10), and even breaking the Sabbath (Numbers 15:32–36). God also made provisions for when people might accidentally kill each other (Numbers 35:9–34). When you look at Scripture as a whole and see the entire context, there are no contradictions.

I could write chapters about how perfect God's Word is and how stories go hand in hand. The Bible is like an intricately woven piece of cloth with every strand linked to every other strand. You can also imagine it as a series of movies. It is as if one writer wrote the first movie and another wrote the sequel without even knowing about the prequel that still another author wrote.

For example, the book of Joshua provides the account of the conquest of Jericho. Jericho was a city with impenetrable walls that God led the Israelites to conquer around 1400 BC. The book of Joshua tells about a prostitute named Rahab. Rahab bravely snuck Israelite spies out of Jericho. It describes Joshua telling the army to rescue only Rahab and her family from the destruction of the city. Then, 1,400 years later, a Jewish tax collector in the Roman Empire named Matthew wrote the genealogy of Jesus. Rahab is a great-great-great-great-great-great-great-grandmother of Jesus.

How does the Bible repeatedly weave different characters and events? The Holy Spirit gave direction and wrote God's story. The Bible is God-breathed (2 Timothy 3:16). Every word of Scripture is His Word.

Prophecy Fulfilled — Internal Evidence #2

The Bible contains many prophecies. A prophecy is not the same as a prediction. When the weather forecaster says there is a 30 percent chance of rain, then there is also a 70 percent chance of no rain. The forecaster is simply making an educated assumption based on mathematical and scientific models, observations, and a knowledge of trends and patterns. During a pre-game show, a sportscaster might predict the final score of a contest based on the strengths and weaknesses of each team. If the final score is different from the sportscaster's guess, which it usually is, no one shouts, "False prophet!" No one threatens the sportscaster with violence. He was only making a prediction.

However, a prophecy contains revelation that declares something about the future. If a prophecy doesn't come true, then the person who stated it is really a "false prophet." God is serious about the integrity of the prophetic word. In Deuteronomy, He says:

> "'But any prophet who falsely claims to speak in my name or who speaks in the name of another god must die.'
>
> "But you may wonder, 'How will we know whether or not a prophecy is from the Lord?' If the prophet speaks in the Lord's name but his prediction does not happen or come true, you will know that the Lord did not give that message. That prophet has spoken without my authority and need not be feared" (Deuteronomy 18:20–22 NLT).

If God has not fulfilled any prophecies of the Bible, it would totally discredit the validity of Scripture. The Old Testament is filled with prophecies about Jesus. They are detailed, specific, and clear, and they are perfectly fulfilled in Jesus Christ. Here are just a few:

1. **Isaiah 7:14 — He would be born of a virgin**: This is one of the most incredible and well-known prophecies. Isaiah prophesied this biological impossibility some 750 years before the birth of Christ. *This prophecy was fulfilled in Luke 1:30–34.*
2. **Micah 5:2 — He would be born in Bethlehem**: Micah lived about 700 years before Jesus and prophesied the city of His birth. This was especially

improbable since Jesus was born in Bethlehem and Bethlehem was such a small city. *This prophecy was fulfilled in Matthew 1:1-2.*

3. **Malachi 3:1 — A forerunner would prepare the Messiah's way.** Malachi gave this prophecy about John the Baptist some 450 years prior to Christ. *This prophecy was fulfilled in Matthew 3:1-3.*

4. **Zechariah 9:9 — The King (Messiah) would come on a colt, the foal of an ass (donkey).** More than 500 years before Christ, Zechariah predicted the method of Jesus' triumphal entry. *This prophecy was fulfilled in Matthew 21:4-5.*

5. **Zech. 11:12 – The price to betray Jesus would be 30 pieces of silver.** *This prophecy was fulfilled in Matthew 26:15.*

6. **Zech. 11:13 — The 30 pieces of silver would eventually go to the potter.** *This prophecy was fulfilled in Matthew 27:3-7.*

7. **Psalm 22:16 — Jesus would be crucified.** Almost 1,000 years before Christ, David predicted specific details of Christ's death—crucifixion. This was 500 years before crucifixion came into practice. *This prophecy was fulfilled in Matthew 27:31-36.*

8. **Psalm 22:18 — They would cast lots for His clothing.** Another verse in this psalm predicted more specific details of the crucifixion, casting lots

for Jesus' clothing. *This prophecy was fulfilled in Matthew 27:35.*

This is just a small sample of the dozens of Old Testament prophecies about Jesus. Most are quoted in several places, so the Old Testament references number in the hundreds. Psalm 22 alone contains numerous prophetic details about Christ.

Can you see how incredible the prophecies of Scripture really are? In the 1950s, Dr. Peter Stoner, the late Professor Emeritus of Science at Westmont College, had his students conduct a study to determine the mathematical probability that even eight biblical prophecies about Jesus could have been fulfilled by one man. They concluded that that the likelihood of Jesus fulfilling even eight prophecies would be 1 in 10 to the 17th power (1 in 100,000,000,000,000,000). *Note that I just listed eight prophecies above.*

To understand the likelihood of this happening, Stoner gave the following illustration:

If you mark one of ten tickets, and place all of the tickets in a hat, and thoroughly stir them, and then ask a blindfolded man to draw one, his chance of getting the right ticket is one in ten. Suppose that we take 10^{17} silver dollars and lay them on the face of Texas. They will cover all of the state two feet deep. Now mark one of these silver dollars and stir the whole mass thoroughly, all over the state. Blindfold a man and tell him that he can travel as far as he wishes, but he must pick up one silver dollar and say that this is the right one. What chance would he have of getting the right one? Just the same chance that the prophets would have had of writing these eight prophecies and having them all come true in any one man, from their day to the present time, providing they wrote using their own wisdom.[5]

You say that's impossible! No, I am saying there is a chance, but it would have to be a total act of God. That's what the Bible is, an act of God.

That's what the Bible is, an act of God.

5. Peter W. Stoner, *Science Speaks, Scientific Proof of the Accuracy of Prophecy and the Bible*, Online Edition revised by Donald W. Stoner (Chicago: Moody Press, 2005), chap. 3, http://sciencespeaks.dstoner.net/ Christ_of_Prophecy.html#c9.

7

Why the Bible? — Part 2

The Resurrection of Jesus — Internal Evidence #3

The Bible records the resurrection of Jesus Christ.
This idea might seem more inconceivable than that of
a virgin birth. Imagine your loved one has died. Even
more, you saw your loved one die. It often takes about
three days to prepare for a modern funeral. On the third
day, you are on your way to view the body when you
begin to hear reports that the casket is empty. At first,
your grief is only multiplied as you try to come to terms
with the body missing. Then one of your friends claims
to have seen your loved one alive and walking down
the road. What emotions would you experience? More
grief? Fear? Anger? Would you think that someone was
playing a cruel trick? Could you even process everything
that is happening?

The Gospel authors say that something very much like
the imagined experience with your loved one happened
with Jesus and His followers. The disciples saw Jesus

beaten. They had seen Him crucified. Some of them stayed until the end when the Roman soldier thrust a spear into Jesus' side and blood and water poured from the wound (John 19:31–34). Jesus was dead—really dead. When the disciples saw everything that happened to Jesus, they ran and hid. They were scared that what was happening to Jesus was going to happen to them. They had no intention of turning the world upside down. They intended to stay alive.

But then, Jesus rose from the dead and spent 40 days with His disciples (Acts 1:3). They saw Him with their own eyes and touched Him with their hands (1 John 1:1). They didn't simply get a glimpse of Him across the lake and say, "Oh, I think that is Jesus." They were so certain of His resurrection that they begin telling everyone He was alive. Their witness led to beatings, imprisonment, and eventually most of them were executed. Very soon after Jesus' resurrection, the Jewish officials arrested some of them and brought them before the Sanhedrin. The Jewish leaders told them to stop telling people that God had resurrected Jesus. The disciples replied, "Do you think God wants us to obey you rather than him?" (Acts 4:19). And when the Jewish officials arrested them again, the disciples' reaction was similar:

> But Peter and the apostles replied, "We must obey God rather than any human authority. The God of our ancestors

raised Jesus from the dead after you killed him by hanging him on a cross. Then God put him in the place of honor at his right hand as Prince and Savior. He did this so the people of Israel would repent of their sins and be forgiven. We are witnesses of these things and so is the Holy Spirit, who is given by God to those who obey him."

When they heard this, the high council was furious and decided to kill them. But one member, a Pharisee named Gamaliel, who was an expert in religious law and respected by all the people, stood up and ordered that the men be sent outside the council chamber for a while. Then he said to his colleagues, "Men of Israel, take care what you are planning to do to these men! Some time ago, there was that fellow Theudas, who pretended to be someone great. About 400 others joined him, but he was killed, and all his followers went their various ways. The whole movement came to nothing. After him, at the time of the census, there was Judas of Galilee. He got people to follow him, but he was killed, too, and all his followers were scattered.

"So my advice is, leave these men alone. Let them go. If they are planning and doing these things merely on their own, it will soon be overthrown. But if it is from God, you will not be able to overthrow them. You may even find yourselves fighting against God!" (Acts 5:29–39 NLT).

A study of early church history reveals that nearly all of those men were eventually executed as martyrs.

According to Tertullian, an early church "father," the apostle John survived boiling in oil, and so Roman authorities exiled him to the island of Patmos.[1] Yet today we still talk about Jesus. Those early Christians died in coliseums, hid in catacombs, and the Emperor Nero would cover them with tar and then light them on fire and place them on posts for his nighttime garden parties. *Foxe's Book of Martyrs* includes the stories of many other men and women who were killed because of their witness for Christ.[2] They all suffered for the cause of a man who never traveled more than 30 miles from His home during His ministry—a man who never wrote any books or owned any property, and who didn't even have a place to rest His own head (Matthew 8:20). Yet the life of Jesus separates time with BC (Before Christ) and AD (*Anno Domini*—the Year of our Lord).[3] Jesus' name is above every other name (Philippians 2:9). The reason for His pre-eminence is that Jesus is the only man to have ever defeated death. And the Bible is the only book that gives the full account of history's greatest event, His resurrection.

---

1. Tracee D. Hackel, "John the Apostle, Critical Issues," ed. John D. Barry et al., *The Lexham Bible Dictionary* (Bellingham, WA: Lexham Press, 2016).
2. John Foxe, *The New Foxe's Book of Martyrs*. Rewritten and updated by Harold J. Chadwick. (North Brunswick, NJ: Bridge-Logos, 1997).
3. "What is the meaning of BC and AD?" https://gotquestions.org/BC-AD.html, accessed October 13, 2016.

The Dead Sea Scrolls — External Evidence #1

Amazingly, the Bible's stories never contradict each other, despite almost 40 authors. Perfectly fulfilled prophecies about Jesus set this book apart from all others. And the Bible's record of His resurrection story has changed the course of history. However, can we really trust the reliability of Scripture? The Bible's individual books were written as much as 3,500 years ago. Do we really have the exact words that the authors wrote so long ago?

Remember, all copies were handwritten. If you had to copy every page of the Old Testament, what are the odds you would make a mistake? They are probably high. Would the people who followed you accurately recopy your version? How many errors would occur? After thousands of years of copying and re-copying, how rare would it be to have the same words today as the original version? Many scholars of antiquity debated this issue and generally held doubt until the discovery of the Dead Sea Scrolls.

In 1947, a boy was throwing rocks into a cave near the northwestern shore of the Dead Sea in an area known as Qumran. Suddenly he heard a sound as if something had broken. He entered the cave and discovered his rocks had hit several clay pots containing some ancient scrolls. Archaeologists soon realized he had discovered approximately 500 ancient manuscripts that were written or copied between 250 BC and AD 68.[4] These manuscripts included fragments of every Old Testament book except Esther, including all of Isaiah and large portions of the Psalms.[5] As biblical scholars compared these ancient manuscripts to existing Hebrew texts, they found almost identical documents. Researchers were astonished. How did the integrity of the Old Testament text remain carefully preserved after so many years? By a miracle, God preserved His Word over the centuries. The Dead Sea Scrolls became the greatest archaeological discovery of the twentieth century. More important for this discussion is that they confirmed the reliability of the Old Testament.

Manuscript Evidence — External Evidence #2

The New Testament's reliability also stands unparalleled to any other document of its era. Over 5,800 Greek New Testament manuscripts exist. This number of manuscripts stands apart from other documents. For example, many people study the works of the great philosophers Aristotle, Socrates, and Plato. The large

---

4. Dr. Shani Tzoref, "Discovery," *The Leon Levy Dead Sea Scrolls — Digital Library* (Israeli Antiquities Authority, 2012), http://www.deadseascrolls.org.il/learn-about-the-scrolls/discovery-and-publication.
5. Avraham Negev, *The Archaeological Encyclopedia of the Holy Land* (New York: Prentice Hall, 1990).

amount of existing manuscripts makes the study of their works possible. However, the numbers of their manuscripts come in a distant second place to the New Testament. There are only a few dozen of their manuscripts in existence combined. The Bible has no equal among ancient books.

The authors of the New Testament all addressed an audience containing many people who lived during the time of the recorded events, and many participated in the events. Imagine if someone today wrote an account of the 9/11 terrorist attack in New York City. If they changed the story and said the World Trade Center buildings were bombed, almost everyone would immediately object to that account. We remember watching, in person or on television, when two planes flew into the two towers. On the other hand, if someone wrote an account of the story 100 years from now, the author might find it easier to persuade people who hadn't lived through the events.

When the apostles and other authors wrote the books of the New Testament, they couldn't fabricate stories because living eyewitnesses would have disputed their claims. The Gospels and the book of Acts were composed and distributed in the same region near the time of the recorded events. Paul tells the ruler Agrippa that nothing they spoke about was done in secret—rather, it was out in the open (Acts 26:26).

Archeological Discoveries — External Evidence #3

The Bible has encountered more than its share of
enemies. Many people have tried to find archeological
evidence to disprove the Bible's accounts. Yet never has
an archaeological discovery satisfactorily refuted any
fact reported in the Bible. In 2007 a well-funded group,
which included James Cameron, director of the 1997
film *Titanic*, claimed that they had found the family
tomb of Jesus. The group financed and produced a documentary. In the end, Amos Kloner, the archeologist who
originally excavated the tomb, and Joe Zias, former cura-
tor of archaeology at the Israeli Antiquities Authority,
reported in the *Jerusalem Post* that the documentary
was "nonsense."[6]

Over time, archaeological discoveries have supported
the Bible's accounts of history, claims about the peoples
and places involved in the stories, and the language
used to describe local customs and historical names. For
example, Genesis describes a great flood that covered the
earth. Many scholars have disputed this account because
they find it hard to believe, partly because it involves a
boat large enough to rescue at least two of every living
creature that existed at the time. However, every ancient
civilization told similar accounts of floodwaters covering
the earth, including the civilizations that had no access

---

6. http://www.jpost.com/Israel/Kloner-A-great-story-but-nonsense, Web.

to the biblical text. The Bible gives witness to people groups such as the Hittites, Canaanites, Perizzites, and Amorites. Archaeologists have discovered evidence of these ancient civilizations within the past 100 years.

Nelson Glueck, an American rabbi and archeologist, said:

> It may be stated categorically that no archaeological discovery has ever controverted a Biblical reference. Scores of archaeological findings have confirmed historical statements of the Bible in clear outline or exact detail. And, by the same token, proper evaluation of Biblical descriptions has often led to amazing discoveries.[7]

A Line in the Sand

I have attempted to cover a large amount of information in the previous two chapters. However, I did this because until you can embrace the reliability of Scripture, you will waver in your trust of its authority. A disciple must decide to obey everything that God commands—even the smallest matters that the enemy tries to attack. Your nature is to make your feelings and thoughts your authority. That is the pattern of the world. If you have never drawn a line in the sand about

7. Josh McDowell, *The New Evidence That Demands a Verdict* (Nashville: Thomas Nelson, 1999), 89.

the authority of God's Word in all things, stop reading, pray, and tell God that you surrender your thoughts and your feelings to Him. My father would always preach in his sermons, "You show me a person who surrenders themselves to the Word of God, and I will show you a person who is secure in the love of God, guarded by His peace, sustained in His joy, and fulfilled in living out His purpose in their lives!" I have learned that God's promises are trustworthy, even in my failures, heartaches, and trials.

I once heard Ravi Zacharias[8] relate a story about a Vietnamese man named Hien Pham.

When Vietnam fell under communist rule, the Vietcong arrested Hien and placed him in prison. His captors only allowed him to read the works of Karl Marx and Friedrich Engels. They forbid him to read in English. After many years of reading *The Communist Manifesto*, his captors convinced him he might be wrong about his views against communism. It seemed to Hien that God had abandoned him, or perhaps there was no God. He decided that he would give up his daily prayer habit when he awoke the next morning.

The next day, the guards assigned Hien the work camp's latrine cleaning duty. He reported that the stench was unimaginable. While cleaning, Hien noticed that one

8. "Ravi Zacharias: Hien Pham" https://soundfaith.com/sermons/28754 -ravi-zacharias-hien-pham.

of the trash buckets contained some excrement-soiled paper with English writing. He pulled it out; and to his astonishment, it contained the complete text of Romans 8. Hien cleaned it off and stuck it in his pocket.

Late that night, with all the lights out, Hien took the sheet out and read it by candlelight:

> Can anything ever separate us from Christ's love? Does it mean he no longer loves us if we have trouble or calamity, or are persecuted, or hungry, or destitute, or in danger, or threatened with death? (As the Scriptures say, "For your sake we are killed every day; we are being slaughtered like sheep.") No, despite all these things, overwhelming victory is ours through Christ, who loved us (Romans 8:35–37 NLT).

Hien's circumstances didn't change, but God's promise of love brought him comfort and peace. He knew God had not abandoned him in that prison camp. When the guards called the roll the next day, Hien asked the soldiers if he could clean the latrines again. They gave him a strange look, but granted his wish. As Hien cleaned, he saw another soiled piece of paper in the trash bucket. He pulled it out, cleaned it off, and placed it in his pocket. That night, Hien lay in bed and read Romans 9.

Every day, Hien volunteered for latrine duty, and day after day he found Scripture in the trash bucket. Apparently, a soldier was using pages from a Bible for toilet paper. Have you ever heard the saying "One man's trash is another man's treasure"? Leaves of paper one man saw as rubbish, God used to restore the heart of a prisoner. Hien treasured God's Word so much that he entered the foulest of places to receive it. Years later, Hien escaped and came to the United States. He said, "I have found there is no longing of the human heart that is satisfied more than knowing the Lord." Ask yourself again, "Do I trust God's Word? Will it get me through any bad thing I might face?"

> "I have found there is no longing of the human heart that is satisfied more than knowing the Lord."

8

Don't Flinch!

Also it does not help that one of you would say: 'I will gladly confess Christ and His Word on every detail, except that I may keep silent about one or two things which my tyrants may not tolerate, such as the form of the Sacraments and the like.' For whoever denies Christ in one detail or word has denied the same Christ in that one detail who was denied in all the details, since there is only one Christ in all His words, taken together or individually. — Martin Luther[1]

When I have the opportunity to speak about topics similar to the previous two chapters, sometimes the smaller issues distract people in the audience. When I finish speaking, some people ask what I think about the Creation versus God working through evolution. Some want to know my opinion about election versus free will. Still others ask when I think Jesus will return, and if it will occur before or after the tribulation.

---

1. *D. Martin Luther's Werke : kritische Gesamtausgabe (Weimarer Ausgabe) : [3. Band] Briefwechsel*, ed. (Weimar: H. Boìˆhlaus Nachfolger, 1933), 81–82.

God intends for us to use our minds, and questions such as these have a place, but we should not become distracted with knowledge simply for the purpose of argument or debate. The enemy loves to get believers caught up in intellectual arguments. In the meantime, those same believers forget to respond to God's promises and they don't let those truths transform their hearts.

The ability to argue boldly for the truth has little value if you cannot be obedient to God's Word when the circumstances of life rage. That is where the battle occurs. There we prove the genuineness of our discipleship. Many believers can declare that they believe all of God's Word, but how do they behave when the enemy attacks? Either they stand firm or they flinch. What circumstances cause you to flinch?

> God intends for us to use our minds, and questions such as these have a place, but we should not become distracted with knowledge simply for the purpose of argument or debate.

When I was a kid, my friends and I thought it was funny to walk up to someone and pretend as if we were going to punch them in the face. Sometimes we would act as if we were going to throw something at them. Then they would fall backward or put their hands in front of their face. We would then all laugh at them. In some ways, we were trying to show that we were bigger or stronger. We would yell, "Made you flinch!" as if that settled the matter. The enemy does something very similar to us. He uses our circumstances so that we will think he is bigger or stronger than we are. When we fall, he laughs and yells, "Made you flinch!"

How does the devil make believers flinch? Here are a few areas I have seen us flinch:

- "I believe the Bible says I am supposed to tithe, but my financial circumstances don't allow me to do it right now."
- "I believe the Bible says I should forgive, but you don't know how much this person hurt me and wronged me."
- "I believe in submitting to godly authority, but I just can't submit to that pastor because he hasn't met my expectations."
- "I believe the Bible says that divorce is wrong, but if you knew what my spouse is like, you would see why I can't be married anymore."
- "I believe the Bible says to think about only those things that are pure and excellent, but other than that one five-minute scene the movie has such a great story and a good message."

- "I know God's Word says to honor my parents, but my parents are pushy and always ask too much of me."

In our world, many Christians don't live out the convictions of their faith. Many people have the excellent ability to argue about certain beliefs or interpretations of Scripture, but that is not the same thing as faith. We can do a good job at professing that we know Christ. The challenge is confessing Christ in those circumstances where it isn't easy to obey His Word. We find it is easier to trust our feelings and thoughts in the moment than it is to trust every promise in Scripture. It is here that we flinch.

Between the Ears and in the Heart

Every battle you ever face will be decided between your ears and in your heart before it is ever won in your circumstances. Consider that statement. What is between your ears? Your mind is. And your heart represents your feelings. You have to win the battle in your thoughts and in your feelings if you are to stand and not flinch in difficult circumstances.

> Every battle you ever face will be decided between your ears and in your heart before it is ever won in your circumstances.

If you love sports, you probably like to watch athletes who become champions. What separates champions from everyone else? The famous boxer, Muhammad Ali, said, "To be a great champion you must believe you are the best. If you're not, pretend you are." He meant that being a champion is something you determine between your ears and in your heart. Based on their experiences and previous victories, boxers like Muhammad Ali or basketball players like Michael Jordan know that they can defeat anyone. They know it in their hearts and minds. They possess a confidence that they have already won the battle before it begins.

Size on the Battlefield

"Don't worry about this Philistine," David told Saul. "I'll go fight him!"

"Don't be ridiculous!" Saul replied. "There's no way you can fight this Philistine and possibly win! You're only a boy, and he's been a man of war since his youth."

But David persisted. "I have been taking care of my father's sheep and goats," he said. "When a lion or a bear comes to steal a lamb from the flock, I go after it with a club and rescue the lamb from its mouth. If the animal turns on me, I catch it by the jaw and club it to death. I have done this to both lions and bears, and I'll do it to this pagan Philistine, too, for he has defied the armies of the living God! The Lord who rescued me from the claws of the lion and the bear will rescue me from this Philistine!"

Saul finally consented. "All right, go ahead," he said. "And may the Lord be with you!" ...

Goliath walked out toward David with his shield bearer ahead of him, sneering in contempt at this ruddy-faced boy. "Am I a dog," he roared at David, "that you come at me with a stick?" And he cursed David by the names of his gods. "Come over here, and I'll give your flesh to the birds and wild animals!" Goliath yelled.

David replied to the Philistine, "You come to me with sword, spear, and javelin, but I come to you in the name of the Lord of Heaven's Armies—the God of the armies of Israel, whom you have defied. Today the Lord will conquer you, and I will kill you and cut off your head. And then I will give the dead bodies of your men to the birds and wild animals, and the whole world will know that there is a God in Israel!" (1 Samuel 17:32–37, 41–46 NLT).

David didn't simply hope God would rescue him when he picked up a few rocks and walked out onto that battlefield. David stood before the king of Israel with confidence, and then he stood before the entire Philistine army with confidence. Finally, he stood before the giant and confidently said, "Today the Lord will conquer you, and I will kill you and cut off your head. Then I am going to take the lives of all your men and feed them to the birds." How was David able to have such confidence? Based on his previous experiences and victories, David knew the power of God could make him a champion. David had already defeated Goliath between his ears and in his heart before he ever pulled out his slingshot.

When I was young, my dad would tell me that I needed to settle who I was and what I was about before I encountered any circumstance in high school or college. "If you don't know who you are, settle it now," he would say. "If you don't settle the issue of what you will do in the circumstance, the moment will always be bigger than you." If I hadn't already decided how I would respond if someone offered me a drink, I would have given into temptation. If I hadn't already determined how far I would go with a girl, I would have definitely gone a lot further. Today, if I don't determine ahead of time to spend time with the Lord in His Word, I will not do it. If I don't determine to bring my tithe and go beyond it as a giver, I won't actually do it. If you don't settle it in your heart, you will give in to your circumstances, and you will flinch.

Daniel was an Israelite whom the Babylonians had taken from his family, his home, and his country. He was then thrown into a very different culture as a prize of war. Because he was of noble birth and very talented, his captors chose him for King Nebuchadnezzar's service. In the book of Daniel he ends up prospering under the reign of at least three kings. The secret to his success is found at the very beginning of the book: "Daniel purposed in his heart that he would not defile himself" (Daniel 1:8 NKJV). Another translation says that Daniel "resolved" (or determined) in his heart not to eat of the king's table. Whether it was standing before a king or standing before the lions, Daniel decided in his heart who he was and what action he would take. He had already settled the matter between his ears and in his heart.

> If you don't settle it in your heart, you will give in to your circumstances, and you will flinch.

If you are going to make it on life's battlefield, you have to settle the matter between your ears and in your heart. You have to confront the issue before the trouble or temptation comes. Resolve who you are in your feelings and thoughts so that you don't flinch when the enemy attacks.

9

A Different Technique

As I mentioned in the Introduction, there are times when we need to rethink the way we do certain things. We may use new methods to replace, improve upon, or supplement the tools we have used in the past. We can now take the fundamental truths that we have learned about the nature of God, God's promises, the authority of the Bible, and how we respond to the world around us, and apply them using this new method—the *Promise Principle.*

Quick Review

And because of his glory and excellence, he has given us great and precious promises. These are the promises that enable you to share his divine nature and escape the world's corruption caused by human desires. In view of all this, make every effort to respond to God's promises. (2 Peter 1:4–5 NLT).

I define the *Promise Principle* as "God's fundamental way to disciple believers through His promises so that we won't participate in our old nature, but instead participate in His divine nature." Your old sin nature simply means you live according to how you feel and think. Those thoughts and feelings are always dictated by the circumstances of life, whether they are troubles or temptations. Once you are saved, your spirit comes to life, and the process of growing in Christ is learning to obey the Spirit. The apostle Peter says that God has given us His promises and if we respond, we can actually participate in His divine nature (2 Peter 1:4).

> I define the *Promise Principle* as "God's fundamental way to disciple believers through His promises so that we won't participate in our old nature, but instead participate in His divine nature."

Role Play

For our example, we will use Philippians 1:1–11. To begin, the group reads aloud the entire chapter, letting each person read a couple verses. The facilitator instructs the group members to underline every promise that they find in the passage. Remember that God's Word is full of two types of promises—truths and commandments—so both types should be underlined. In our example below, several promises have been underlined.

This letter is from Paul and Timothy, <u>slaves of Christ Jesus.</u>

I am writing to all of <u>God's holy people</u> in Philippi <u>who belong to Christ Jesus,</u> including the elders and deacons.

<u>May God our Father and the Lord Jesus Christ give you grace and peace.</u>

Every time I think of you, I give thanks to my God. Whenever I pray, I make my requests for all of you with joy, for you have been my <u>partners in spreading the Good News about Christ</u> from the time you first heard it until now. And I am certain that God, <u>who began the good work within you, will continue his work until it is finally finished</u> on the day when Christ Jesus returns.

So it is right that I should feel as I do about all of you, for you have a special place in my heart. <u>You share with me the special favor of God,</u> both in my imprisonment and in defending and confirming the truth of the Good News. God knows how much I love you and long for you with the tender compassion of Christ Jesus.

<u>I pray that your love will overflow more and more, and that you will keep on growing in knowledge and understanding. For I want you to understand what really matters, so that you may live pure and blameless lives until the day of</u>

Christ's return. <u>May you always be filled with the fruit of</u>
<u>your salvation</u> —the righteous character produced in your
life by Jesus Christ—<u>for this will bring much glory and</u>
<u>praise to God</u> (Philippians 1:1–11 NLT).

After reading, the facilitator tells the group to begin
with the first five verses and asks if anyone wants to
respond to a promise. One person jumps in and says,
"I underlined verse 2!" The following is a sample
conversation:

Facilitator: Okay, go ahead and read it again for us.
Person 1: "May God our Father and the Lord Jesus
   Christ give you grace and peace."
Facilitator: Why did you underline that verse?
Person 1: Paul is asking God to give the people of
   Philippi grace and peace. So if Paul is asking for it, I
   want to ask for it.
Facilitator: What is an area in your life right now that
   needs God's grace and peace?
Person 1: You know, right now is tax season, and I am
   an accountant. There is so much going on in my head,
   and I am working with so many different people that I
   can easily get overwhelmed.
The facilitator then asks him to respond to the promise of grace and peace in this verse. We should do
"everything by prayer" (Philippians 4:6), so the facilitator

instructs him to pray with his eyes open. He can look at this verse as he is praying and talk to God about what is in his heart.

Person 1: Dear Lord, You know everything that is going on in my life right now. I am stressed right now and feel overwhelmed. Lord, I need Your grace today as I make decisions and work on these files. I ask that You fill my mind with Your peace that I wouldn't be frazzled. My trust is in You, Jesus. Amen.

Facilitator: Great job Person 1!

Person 2: I underlined verse 5! It says, "You have been my partners in spreading the Good News about Christ from the time you first heard it until now."

Facilitator: Why did you underline that verse?

Person 2: You know, as we were reading, this truth just jumped out to me. It says we are partners in spreading the good news. A lot of times, I buy the lie that ministry and talking to people about God are just for the pastor. I think, "I'm just a plumber, and God can't use me." But here Paul is telling the people that they are just as much a part of spreading the gospel as he was.

Facilitator: Is this something you need to ask God for by faith or receive with thanksgiving?

Person 2: Both!

Facilitator: Okay, go ahead and respond to the promise. Pray it!

Person 2: Dear heavenly Father, I thank You for Your truth that we are partners in sharing the gospel. I know that I buy the lie so many times that I am just a plumber, but I receive this truth in my heart. Lord, You have put a calling on my heart to share Your love. I ask that You would give me boldness and eyes to see opportunities for me to minister to people as I work. In Jesus' name, Amen.

From Your Head to Your Heart

In our *Promise Principle* groups, we tell people to read the verse and explain it, because one way we process information is by saying things aloud. As people explain the parts of the passage they have underlined and the circumstances they are confronting, they are processing information about this promise.

The apostle John says that the Holy Spirit guides us into all truth (John 16:13). When you are listening to a sermon or reading a passage of Scripture and something touches your spirit so that you think, "Oh, that is good," that can't be your reasoning alone. You don't qualify something as good—only God is good, so only He can qualify something as good. Remember, if you can't even say, "Jesus is Lord" without the Holy Spirit (1 Corinthians 12:3), then you can't be guided into truth without the Spirit. You must understand that the Holy Spirit is speaking to you when you recognize truth.

The Holy Spirit teaches you to recognize truth in your mind right at that moment. So we ask you to pray through it. Why do we do that? Because we want you to engage that truth with your spirit. When you pray that truth, you are actually allowing that thought in your head to move into your heart. This is important because it puts the truth in the center of your feelings.

> Your word I have hidden in my heart, that I might not sin against You (Psalm 119:11 NKJV).

As long as the truth stays in your head, it is just information. Once it gets into your heart, it becomes transformation.

> As long as the truth stays in your head, it is just information. Once it gets into your heart, it becomes transformation.

In Spirit and In Truth

But the time is coming—indeed it's here now—when true worshipers will worship the Father in spirit and in truth. The Father is looking for those who will worship him that way. For God is Spirit, so those who worship him must worship in spirit and in truth. (John 4:23–24 NLT).

Jesus is visiting with a Samaritan woman. She tries to debate with Him about the appropriate place of worship. She focuses on information. The woman recognized Jesus as a prophet, so she wanted to have a theological discussion. I believe many of us try to handle the things of God with only our minds. We feel safe that way, because nothing in our life has to change. We like to know facts and theological stances, and we like to obtain more truth. But Jesus isn't interested in head knowledge by itself; He wants to lead us into transformation. So Jesus responds to the woman by telling her that it isn't where you worship but how you worship that matters. He tells her that God is Spirit, and we are to worship Him in spirit and in truth. It isn't merely with your head; it must include your heart. I don't believe that Jesus was simply referring to the way we sing in worship. He was talking about how we engage God in every aspect of our life—in spirit and in truth. He also wants us to engage the Word of God in spirit and in truth.

Consider the way we sometimes conduct our Bible studies. We gather to study God's Word or follow a book that someone wrote about God's Word. Someone opens with prayer, another gives instruction, and then we discuss truths with each other, sharing what we think about the passage. Then close in prayer and leave with more information.

Now imagine you attend a friend's birthday party. When you arrive, you greet the birthday friend, but after saying hello, you never engage with him again. You sit around with the other birthday guests and talk about your friend. You tell the others what you like about him and maybe learn some more facts about him, but never talk to him. At the end of the party, you walk up and say goodbye to your birthday friend. Don't you think that would be disappointing for the birthday boy? Isn't that how we often do Bible study? We arrive and greet God with an opening prayer, talk about Him for 45 minutes, and then say goodbye to Him with a closing prayer asking Him to bless everyone.

You see, God created my spirit to relate to Him. My spirit is the eternal part of me. When I sing to Him or when I talk to Him in prayer, my spirit leads this communion. In our *Promise Principle* groups, we want to be talking to God throughout the study. In fact, there is often a joke in our groups that if you talk about a passage, you end by praying it. We don't just talk about the promises of God, we respond to God's promises through prayer, by receiving with thanksgiving, and asking by faith. This type of study allows God's truth to move from merely intellectual information to transformational power in your soul. It is amazing how it gives space for the Holy Spirit to deal with you personally and teach you what He wants you to hear from His Word. As you encounter God's Word in spirit and in truth, it no longer is just information. And you become not just a hearer of God's Word, but also a doer of God's Word (James 1:22).

Let me also add that as you pray and respond to God's Word with your spirit, God hides His truth in the center of your feelings (Psalm 119:11). This is the way God renews your thoughts and attitudes (Romans 12:2). God promises that when you bring all things to Him in prayer, He will fill you with peace (Philippians 4:6). Moreover, peace involves your feelings. God will begin to give you a feeling of peace on certain matters, and a lack of peace on other matters. The more your spirit matures, the more you will notice these important differences.

Responding to the Promise

Let's look at the rest of the passage we read earlier and explore one more promise from Philippians 1:1–11.

I pray that your love will overflow more and more, and that you will keep on growing in knowledge and understanding. For I want you to understand what really matters, so that you may live pure and blameless lives until the day of Christ's return. May you always be filled with the fruit of your salvation—the righteous character produced in your life by Jesus Christ—<u>for this will bring much glory and</u> <u>praise to God</u> (Philippians 1:9–11 NLT).

Facilitator: Did anyone underline anything here?

Person 3: I actually underlined three verses together because Paul is praying here for the people of Philippi.

Facilitator: Why did you underline it? What circumstance does God want to speak about in your life?

The man explains that he and his wife have been struggling. He can't understand his wife, and nothing he ever does seems to be enough. His wife can make him lose his temper so easily. Then he finds himself being unkind to her, and doesn't even know if he can love her anymore as he once did.

Facilitator: What is the promise in this prayer?

Person 3: I remember when we were studying Romans 5:5: "He has given us the Holy Spirit to fill our hearts with his love" (NLT). Paul asked God to let their love overflow, so I know that is a work of the Holy Spirit in my life to be able to love more and more. I also need God to help me understand what really matters in my marriage and not fight over such petty things. So I need Him to fill me with His presence so that I will be filled with the fruit of the Spirit.

Facilitator: It sounds like you are saying you need to ask in faith for this promise. Go ahead and pray it.

Person 3: "Dear heavenly Father, I thank You for Your promises and that You give me what I need to be a godly husband. I submit myself to You and ask You to fill me with Your love, so that I would overflow with love for my wife. I ask that You would help me to understand the things that really matter. Help me to live pure and blameless. Would you fill me with the fruit of Your salvation, so that I would have self-control and kindness when I am talking to my wife? I want the way I treat my wife to bring You praise and glory. In Jesus name I pray, Amen."

Memorizing with Your Spirit

I still remember the first time a man at a *Promise Principle* group said to me, "So that's how you do that!" At first, I didn't understand what he was talking about, and so I replied, "That's how I do what?" He replied that he often wondered how I could pull other Scriptures out of my head when we were studying a different passage. He soon found he could do the same thing. (That is what Person 3 was doing in the example with Romans 5:5.) What he was experiencing was the Holy Spirit recalling other verses that he had hidden in his heart, because he had been praying them as promises so much.

My parents required me to memorize Scripture while I was growing up. I would write verses on index cards and memorize one verse per week, so I have always been able to recall Scripture. However, since I began praying God's promises, I have memorized far more Scripture with my spirit than with my head. That is what happens with many people when they start responding to the Bible with their spirits rather than merely with their minds. It is a great blessing when I hear people cross-reference other promises from God's Word as God is speaking to them about a promise we are reading together.

Lifting Up a Standard

> When the enemy comes in like a flood,
> The Spirit of the Lord will lift up a standard against him.
> (Isaiah 59:19b NKJV).

God made His Word alive and active (Hebrews 4:12), giving it the ability to bring life and healing to your whole body (Proverbs 4:22). One of God's greatest promises is that the Holy Spirit will bring forth His Word in you when the enemy comes against you. But His word won't be lifted up in you and against the enemy's flood if the Word isn't in you. Many of us spend more time reading Christian books by famous authors than we do reading the Bible. If you disciple anyone, it can't consist primarily of books written by other people. Christian books can be aids, but the Word of God must be the source. When trouble or temptation comes, an inspiring quote from an ordinary book will not rise up within you.

James says, "Submit to God. Resist the devil and he will flee from you" (James 4:7 NKJV). We often struggle with submitting to God because it means submitting to what He says. If you haven't hidden His Word in your heart, you can't submit to God in the moment. Then you won't be able to resist the devil in that circumstance, and the flood will overtake you.

> Christian books can be aids, but the Word of God must be the source.

I have come to believe this technique is the fastest and most efficient way to plant God's promises deep in people's hearts. Peter said that we need to grow (2 Peter 3:18). If you don't follow a method like this one, you may have a great amount of knowledge, but you will continue to live as though you were never saved (2 Peter 1:9). I know that I am using strong words, but Peter said—and, more importantly, the Holy Spirit said, "The more you grow like this, the more productive and useful you will be in your knowledge of our Lord Jesus Christ. But those who fail to develop in this way are shortsighted or blind, forgetting that they have been cleansed from their old sins" (2 Peter 1:8–9 NLT).

Promise Principle Group Format

In our *Promise Principle* groups at Gateway Church, we study one book of the Bible at a time. If we are studying 1 John, we look at one chapter each week. The group reads the passage together as each person underlines the promises of God in that chapter. We respond to the promises that we have found by reading aloud the verses we underlined. Then we pray them aloud. As a group and as individuals, we ask by faith or receive the promise with thanksgiving—often both. The truth that the Holy Spirit teaches from His Word transforms lives. Great power comes from studying in a group because each individual learns from the Holy Spirit by listening to other members of the group.

After each study session, the facilitator encourages the group members to continue with the same technique in their personal quiet time. Every day, members read the next chapter, underlining the promises of God that they find, and then respond to them during their time with the Lord. Some people like to use a different translation every day, perhaps using a Bible application on their cell phone or computer Bible software. The goal is not to merely read the chapter and underline the verses. We hope the group members will let the Holy Spirit speak to each of them through His Word, pray the verses that they underline, and then write (perhaps in a journal) about what He teaches them.

The next week, we read the following chapter. We will study 1 John for five weeks, because that is the number of chapters in the book. If group members spend their own time with the Lord at least five days a week, they will have read and prayed through every chapter at least five times, each time praying God's promises. Imagine taking meat and letting it soak in a marinade so that it works down deep. When people marinate in the promises of 1 John for five weeks, God takes all those promises and hides them in their hearts. That way, when the enemy comes like a flood, the Spirit of the Lord will raise that standard (or promise) up within them.

After just five weeks, I have seen new believers gain the ability to share deep spiritual things from the book of 1 John. They might not have a lot of experience with God's Word yet, but if someone is going through a difficulty or trial they can already pray and help that person respond to the promises of God.

My Favorite Testimonial

I encourage you to try this technique. Read a passage of Scripture and underline every promise you encounter.

Decide whether each promise is a *truth or a command-ment*. Then ask the Lord how you should respond to the promise. Do you need to ask God by faith to give you the ability to follow His commandment? Or should you receive His truth with thankfulness? Then pray the Scripture and write down what the Holy Spirit puts on your heart. I also encourage you to get into a *Promise Principle* group or form a group of your own. It will transform your life.

I have personally witnessed how much this technique can affect someone's life. My father-in-law sent me this text one Thanksgiving morning:

> Been giving this some thought recently. I have had four events that have shaped my life in the most significant ways over the past 62 years: 1. My acceptance of Jesus into my heart as the Lord and Savior of my life in 1967. 2. My marriage to Susie Griffin Ruth in 1974. 3. Our trip to Israel in 2009—it made my Bible go from black and white to color. 4. Using the *Promise Principle* both to study the Bible and in my quiet time/prayer time. I'm blessed by you for so many reasons ... taking care of our daughter Shelly, and your five beautiful children, and watching you use the many gifts that God has given you! I love you. Rob

When I received this text, I didn't even know that my father-in-law was in a *Promise Principle* group or that he was using it to study his Bible. I was amazed and humbled that my father-in-law, a godly and influential man, would list this technique as one of the four most important events that have shaped his life. I couldn't market it better than that. Thanks, Pops!

10

Promises Are Weapons

My parents had three children, all boys. I am the oldest. My brother Josh and I did everything together growing up. We played together and got in trouble together—everything was together because we were born only 20 months apart. My youngest brother, Matt, was 9 years younger than I was; when I left home for college, he was only in the third grade. He really had a different experience growing up because he lived like an only child after Josh and I left the house. Mom and Dad would tell us they practiced parenting on their two older boys and then were perfect parents for Matt.

Even though there was such an age difference, Josh and I have always looked up to Matt. He always knew who he was and how he would live his life. In fact, even when Matt was a teenager, I would tell people he was like Joseph in the Old Testament. The Bible says several times that those around Joseph could tell that God's hand was upon him. Matt had, and still has, God's favor on him. He boldly lived for Christ in a large public high school. His peers loved him, his teachers adored him, and his classmates elected him homecoming king during his senior year. I do not exaggerate when I say he saw more than a hundred friends become followers of Christ during those years.

Matt was the person who really showed me the power of this method for studying the Bible. He was a student pastor in a local church when he began studying in this way. When he first started his position in that church, he discovered that the students said they loved Jesus and knew all the Sunday school answers, but they had no fruit in their lives. They seemed dead and defeated by their circumstances rather than alive in the victory that belonged to them in Christ.

Matt began seeking the Lord, asking, "What was different in my life in high school that allowed me to walk in the victory of Jesus rather than the defeat of my sin and insecurities?" It was then that the Holy Spirit reminded him of 2 Peter 1:3–4, a passage our dad loved to quote to us when we were growing up. Matt realized that knowing and responding to the promises of God allowed him to participate in the nature of God and live in victory rather than according to his sinful nature.

So Matt started a Bible study in his apartment that he called Next Level. He and five high school young men read the book of James, underlining and praying the promises of God. Over the next year, a revival began in their student ministry. Many students came to know Christ, many of their friends came to Christ, and other students who had been living in a dead and defeated way became alive and contagious in their passion for God and other people. Many of those students have gone on to lead their own Next Level groups when they moved or went to college.

As Matt was sharing with me everything he was learning, God was also teaching me an understanding of the body, soul, and spirit. He was teaching me how He could transform my soul (mind), and He was showing me about the patterns of the world. I no longer had to conform to those patterns. (Romans 12:2) Earlier I shared some of my story, and told about how I had been hurt in the church. As I struggled with authority, I realized how that experience had crippled me in my spiritual journey. God began teaching me that I had to settle the issue of authority in my life. All of these things began to come together as God taught me to respond to His promises. *Then came the football game.*

A Question of Weapons

On January 12, 2013, the Baltimore Ravens played the Denver Broncos in the American Football Conference Championship game. They played the game in Denver because Peyton Manning and the Broncos had been the dominant team all year, and their record gave them home field advantage. The Ravens were playing with high emotion because their standout player, Ray Lewis, had announced that he would be retiring from the game at the end of the season. So if the Ravens lost, it would be Lewis's last game. Lewis was a team leader, and in my humble opinion, one of the top three linebackers ever to play in the National Football League. I don't recall ever seeing another player perform with more passion than Lewis. His emotion raised the level of play of every man on his team.

With no timeouts and 31 seconds left in the game, the Ravens had the ball 70 yards away from scoring, and they needed a touchdown just to tie the game. In case you are not a fan of American football, those are dire circumstances, and the game appeared to be over. All the Broncos needed to do was prevent a score for two or three plays.

Then, on third down and 3 yards to go, Ravens quarterback Joe Flacco threw a long-distance pass down the sideline to wide receiver Jacoby Jones. Jones had slipped behind the defense and had placed himself at least five yards behind the Broncos' defenders when he caught the ball. He ran into the end zone for a touchdown and silenced the home crowd who thought they were only a few plays from celebrating a trip to the Super Bowl. The

Ravens tied the game. Then they ended up winning in double overtime on a field goal kick.

After the game, as the players were running off the field, a sports reporter stopped Ray Lewis. First, he gave God the glory for the win. Then he shared a thought he said the Lord kept giving him while he was playing with some injuries during the season. The reporter asked Lewis, "Why did you believe that you were going to win that game?" Lewis passionately responded: "No weapon forged against me shall prosper! No weapon forged against me shall prosper!"

My first thought was, "I don't think that verse in Isaiah 54:17 is addressing the AFC Championship game." But then I felt as if the Lord was asking me a question: "Why do the weapons of the enemy seem to prosper against my people?" Many people claim to love God, yet they don't look any different from the rest of the world when they face troubles and temptation. Some of us believers can look quite defeated and overwhelmed by the onslaught of the enemy. We live as though we are powerless and confused; not according to the promise that "overwhelming victory is ours through Christ, who loved us" (Romans 8:37 NLT). The apostle Paul says, "It is for freedom that Christ has set us free," but it also says we can let ourselves "be burdened again by a yoke of slavery" (Galatians 5:1 NIV). It is possible to walk in freedom, but so many of us have returned to a yoke of slavery.

If it is true that no weapon can be forged against us, why does it appear as if the enemy's weapons are prospering? Do you feel like they are prospering against you? God made it possible for you and me that they won't prosper against us. God has given us stronger weapons.

Lassoing Stray Cattle

For though we live in the world, we do not wage war as the world does. The weapons we fight with are not the weapons of the world. On the contrary, they have divine power to demolish strongholds. We demolish arguments and every pretension that sets itself up against the knowledge of God, and we take captive every thought to make it obedient to Christ (2 Corinthians 10:3–5 NIV).

I memorized this passage in high school because I struggled with lustful thoughts, as many young people do. I knew I needed to take captive any impure thoughts. I really didn't know what that meant at the time. So I pictured myself lassoing thoughts as if I were a cowboy trying to catch stray cattle in a pasture. The cattle were the random impure thoughts that seemed to jump into my head out of nowhere. Over time, I learned more about what it meant to take my thoughts captive and make them obedient to Christ.

Our weapons are all the promises of God that you read about previously. If you will respond to and grab hold of His promises you can resist the enemy's argument and make your feelings and thoughts obedient to Christ. Instead of obeying your sinful nature that is responding to circumstances, God will help you participate in His divine nature.

> Our weapons are all the promises of God that you read about previously.
> If you will respond to and grab hold of His promises you can resist the enemy's argument and make your feelings and thoughts obedient to Christ.

On one occasion, I was drinking coffee with a man who had lost his job. His marriage was also troubled, and he was full of fear and anxiety. I asked him to identify the enemy's argument that was being set up against the knowledge of God. He thought for a moment and said, "That it is my job to provide for my family and I can't do it. That I married the wrong person and it would be better simply to quit. That it is up to me to fix everything and it's all over my head."

So I replied, "If those are the enemy's arguments in your thoughts and feelings, what is the knowledge of

God that opposes them?" The man thought about my question for a second and said, "God's Word promises that God is my provider and He will supply all my needs (Philippians 4:19). God's Word says if I seek Him first, everything will be added unto me (Matthew 6:33). God's Word says to not be anxious in anything but to bring it to Him in prayer (Philippians 4:6)."

I asked him if he wanted to respond to those promises rather than being overwhelmed in his circumstances. He immediately bowed his head right there in the coffee shop and prayed:

"Dear Lord, I am feeling overwhelmed right now. I have lost my job and I don't think I can last in this marriage. I thank you that you are my provider and you are faithful to supply all my needs. I put my trust in You. I want to stop focusing on all the things that are making me anxious. I seek you first. Would you change my heart and do a work in me? My heart is yours and I thank you for taking away my anxiety and giving me peace. I love you. Amen."

I didn't have to deliver any advice to that man; God had already done it. All I had to do was ask him to identify the enemy's arguments and God's answers. The Holy Spirit spoke to him and raised the standard that he had hidden in his heart. The man responded in prayer and made his thoughts and feelings obedient to Christ. His circumstances hadn't changed, but he was filled with peace and walking in faith. He also walked away knowing that it wasn't me who gave him the instruction—the Holy Spirit had been his Counselor. How much better is it for someone to hear from God than to hear from another person?

That man loved the Lord but had lost heart and felt overwhelmed. The enemy was forging weapons against him, but because he had hidden God's truth in his heart, he was immediately able to hear the Holy Spirit and take his thoughts captive. The result was the promise that the enemies' weapons didn't prosper against him. He simply needed another believer to listen and help him for a moment.

Restoring the Sparkle to Your Eyes

O Lord, how long will you forget me? Forever?
How long will you look the other way?
How long must I struggle with anguish in my soul,
with sorrow in my heart every day?
How long will my enemy have the upper hand?

Turn and answer me, O Lord my God!
Restore the sparkle to my eyes, or I will die.
Don't let my enemies gloat, saying, "We have defeated him!"
Don't let them rejoice at my downfall.

159

But I trust in your unfailing love.

I will rejoice because you have rescued me.

I will sing to the Lord

because he is good to me (Psalm 13:1–6 NLT).

Many times in my life I have prayed: "God, where are You? Have You completely forgotten me?" At times, I have felt like I had sorrow in my heart all day long. David says, "I feel like the sparkle in my eye is gone, and I think I am going to die." I have never felt that I was going to die, but maybe you have. David wrote while he was in the middle of a circumstance that was killing his soul and he thought he was physically going to die.

If we were to sit with King David, as I did with the man who had recently lost his job, we would say, "What is the argument that is setting itself up against the knowledge of God in you?" David would say, "It seems God has forgotten me. He doesn't even care and has turned His back on me, because my circumstances aren't changing. The enemy has defeated me, and I am going to die."

Then our reply would be, "So what is the knowledge of God that is being opposed by the enemy?" David would think about it and reply, "God loves me, and His love never fails. He is my rescuer, and He is good." Now the only thing to do is make that thought obedient to Christ, so David would pray: "Dear God, I have felt anguish in my heart and am totally defeated, but I trust in Your unfailing love. I will rejoice because You have rescued me. I sing to you, Lord, because You are so good to me. Amen."

I love reading the Psalms because most of them are prayers or songs written out of the composer's circumstances. The author is responding with the promises of God, even though the circumstances haven't changed. David didn't need us to walk him through those questions, because in his spiritual maturity God had taught him to take those thoughts captive and make them align with what he knew about God.

In fact, every story in Scripture involves someone who is allowing circumstance to rule or is walking in God's promise and living by faith. If they were able to live by faith, it means they had to act on the promises that God had given them, despite what they felt or thought. Here are just a few of the people of faith whom the Bible mentions. I can't imagine the emotions, the fears, and the unknowns in each of their circumstances.

> In fact, every story in Scripture involves someone who is allowing circumstance to rule or is walking in God's promise and living by faith.

- **Job** had lost his children and everything he owned (Job 1).
- **Noah** had a huge boat to build and a family to save (Genesis 6:9–16).
- **Abraham** was old, with no children, and God asked him to leave everything he knew (Genesis 12–21).
- **Joseph** was sold into slavery, falsely accused, and imprisoned (Genesis 37–39).
- **Moses** was told to go and tell Pharaoh to let the Israelites leave Egypt (Exodus 4–14).
- **Joshua** had a river to cross at flood stage and a city to conquer (Joshua 3–6).
- **Rahab** faced helping spies escape her city, even if it meant betraying her own people—and the fear of what could happen if she were caught (Joshua 2).
- **Gideon** led an army of 300 to face the Midianites and Amalekites, who were more numerous than a swarm of locusts (Judges 7).
- **David** faced a giant who had never experienced defeat and a king who believed him to be a traitor (1 Samuel 17–31).
- **Esther** married a Persian king and had to out-maneuver a man who wanted to annihilate her people (Esther 3–5).
- **Jeremiah** foresaw the coming judgment of his people who refused to listen (Jeremiah 7:27).

- **Daniel** was told he couldn't pray to anyone but the king and was thrown into a den of lions (Daniel 6).
- **Hosea** had a wife who prostituted herself (Hosea 1–3).
- **Mary** was pregnant outside of marriage and faced a community that wouldn't understand her miracle. (Luke 1–2, Matthew 1).
- **Jesus** emptied himself of everything, took the form of a man, took the sin and sickness of the world upon himself, and died on the cross (Philippians 2:6–8).

We know the circumstances of all these people and the ways they responded to God's promises. They are examples of faith. Jesus is the ultimate example. His circumstances were the most challenging, but the Bible says that He was obedient even unto death (Philippians 2:8) and that, for the joy set before Him, He endured the cross and scorned its shame (Hebrews 12:2). Jesus took hold of the promise of the Father's master plan that would bring salvation to every human being. Because of His obedience, the Bible says He was given the name above every name and at His name one day every knee should bow and confess that He is Lord (Philippians 2:10–11).

What circumstances continually overwhelm you? God wants you to know that "despite all these things, overwhelming victory is ours through Christ, who loved us." (Romans 8:37 NLT). No matter what you are going through, you can have overwhelming victory. If you feel defeated and that you have lost the sparkle in your eye, you must do what David did: You have to grab hold of God's promises, the knowledge of God, and take your circumstance to God in prayer and make that situation obedient to Christ. God's promises are His weapons, and they are awesome in power. They can destroy anything that the enemy tries to forge against you. But you must take hold of your weapon.

> God's promises are His weapons, and they are awesome in power. They can destroy anything that the enemy tries to forge against you. But you must take hold of your weapon.

11

Grab Your Weapon

Not that I have already obtained all this, or have already arrived at my goal, but I press on to take hold of that for which Christ Jesus took hold of me. Brothers and sisters, I do not consider myself yet to have taken hold of it. But one thing I do: Forgetting what is behind and straining toward what is ahead, I press on toward the goal to win the prize for which God has called me heavenward in Christ Jesus (Philippians 3:12–14 NIV).

Perhaps you have seen the movie *Indiana Jones and the Last Crusade*. The story focuses on the search for the Holy Grail, the legendary cup from which Jesus drank at the Last Supper. Indiana's father, Dr. Henry Jones, made it his life's goal to find the Grail. Henry has been kidnapped, so Indiana uses his father's diary, along with the help of Dr. Elsa Schneider (who is actually a Nazi agent), to track down his father and the Grail. They face many perils and survive multiple harrowing events that would have killed an ordinary person.

At the end of the movie, they have the Holy Grail in their hands, but Elsa inadvertently sets off an earthquake when she starts to take the Grail past a great seal in the floor of the temple where the Grail has been hidden. The Grail tumbles into a crevasse, and Indiana barely catches Elsa when she also falls into it. As she strains to reach the Grail, Indiana yells at her to give him her other hand, but she disregards him and plummets into the abyss. Indiana then falls into the same pit, but his father manages to catch his hand. Indiana too grasps desperately at the Grail, but when his father tells him, "Let it go," he grabs his father's hand, and they escape from the collapsing temple.[1]

Paul wrote that he is "[taking] hold of that for which Christ Jesus took hold of me" (Philippians 3:12 NIV). He is reaching out the way Indiana reached out for his father's hand. When we come to Christ, He grabs hold of us, but growing in Christ requires us to grab hold of Him and everything He saved us for. People who don't do this "fail to develop" and are "shortsighted or blind, forgetting that they have been cleansed from their old sins" (2 Peter 1:9 NLT). What are you reaching for right now? Do you feel like you are slipping or secure? Are you grabbing hold of God's promises or the things of this world?

---

1. Steven Spielberg, *Indiana Jones and The Last Crusade* (Los Angeles: Paramount Pictures, 1989), Film.

Get a Grip!

Do not love the world or the things in the world. If anyone loves the world, the love of the Father is not in him. For all that is in the world—the lust of the flesh, the lust of the eyes, and the pride of life—is not of the Father but is of the world. And the world is passing away, and the lust of it; but he who does the will of God abides forever (1 John 2:15–17 NKJV).

God has given us all of His promises so that we can live according to His nature and "[escape] the corruption *that is* in the world through lust" (2 Peter 1:4 NKJV). To love God means you obey everything that He has commanded. If you continue to reach for the things of this world, you really don't have the love of the Father in you. To run for God, to love God, to grab hold of all that He has saved you for, is to grab hold of His promises so that you can win the prize for which He is calling you heavenward. "Then God will give you a grand entrance into the eternal Kingdom of our Lord and Savior Jesus Christ" (2 Peter 1:11 NLT).

When I was growing up, we would use a particular phrase when someone was being overly emotional: "Get a grip!" It means to grab hold of reality. Nothing is more real than the promises of God. His truth and His commandments are the reality that will bring us life and peace. God's promises are the weapons with which we fight. They can knock down any stronghold (2 Corinthians 10:4). They are the "anchor for our souls" (Hebrews 6:19 NLT). However, if you don't have a strong grip on God's promises, they can't anchor your life in the middle of the storm.

Imagine you are a warrior with a mighty weapon. You have a sword that can destroy any enemy. What good is that weapon if you don't know how to use it? What if your grip isn't strong enough to hold onto it when your enemy attacks you? Your enemy has a strategy to defeat you—he wants to knock that weapon out of your grip. Do you know the strength of your grip on the promises of God? Take time to evaluate yourself. I will use your five fingers to represent the disciplines that you need in order to grab hold of the promises of God.

Finger #1 — Hearing the Word from Others

> So then faith *comes* by hearing, and hearing by the word of God (Romans 10:17 NKJV).

When you go to church and hear the preacher deliver the Word of God, you have an opportunity to hear the truth. You can hear sermons that will challenge you to live the Christian life. The preacher supplies applications and illustrations to help you better understand how to obey. That is the key, because it isn't just about hearing the Word. Faith comes from hearing *and* obeying (*shema*) the Word of God. You must learn to be a doer of the Word (James 1:22). Growth in Christ begins with hearing the Word of God so that you can obey it.

If you are actively hearing and obeying the Word, you are doing the right thing. This is where you must begin. However, if this is where you stop—if all you do every week is go to church and hear the Word—you will live spiritually weak. I want you to imagine that you are trying to grab your sword with only one finger. Can you grab your Bible and hold it with only one finger? You can't really grab your Bible that way. Try to balance it on your index finger. Don't cheat by using your palm to brace it. How much opposition would it take to knock that Bible out of your hand? A small gust of wind would probably knock it from your hand.

> Now the serpent was more cunning than any beast of the field which the Lord God had made. And he said to the woman, "Has God indeed said, 'You shall not eat of every tree of the garden'?"
>
> And the woman said to the serpent, "We may eat the fruit of the trees of the garden; but of the fruit of the tree which *is* in the midst of the garden, God has said, 'You shall not eat it, nor shall you touch it, lest you die.'"

Then the serpent said to the woman, "You will not surely die. For God knows that in the day you eat of it your eyes will be opened, and you will be like God, knowing good and evil" (Genesis 3:1–5 NKJV).

Satan plots to knock the Word right out of your hand. He always attacks the Word of God first. Genesis says, "Then the Lord God took the man and put him in the Garden of Eden to tend and keep it. And the Lord God commanded the man, saying, 'Of every tree of the garden you may freely eat; but of the tree of the knowledge of good and evil you shall not eat, for in the day that you eat of it you shall surely die'" (Genesis 2:15–17 NKJV). At some point Satan came to Eve and said, "Did God really say, 'You shall not eat of every tree of the garden?'" Satan attacks the actual words of God; he exaggerates them and twists them.

Eve replies that God commanded, "You shall not eat it, nor shall you touch it, lest you die." Did you notice that Eve was confused about the command? God had said nothing about not touching the fruit—He had only said, "Don't eat it."

But can you really blame Eve? To whom did God give the commandment? Adam! And maybe Adam told her correctly. However, if you get the Word of God *only* from other people, you may be prone to confusion.

Job speaks of the key to avoiding this confusion, "For the ear tests words as the tongue tastes food. Let us discern for ourselves what is right; let us learn together what is good" (Job 34:3–4 NIV). The key to the next level of grabbing hold of God's Word is discernment. We gain the ability to discern God's Word when we study it and share it. Paul says, "And this I pray, that your love may abound still more and more in knowledge and all discernment, that you may approve the things that are excellent, that you may be sincere and without offense till the day of Christ" (Philippians 1:9–10 NKJV). That is how we get a better grip.

Finger #2 — Study the Word for Yourself

Deep down we know that sermons and teachings, although edifying, can never replace the carrying power we find when we sit at His feet and hear His word for ourselves.[2]

One of the most important disciplines any of us can do is develop a daily time of being in God's Word for ourselves. David said,

---

2. Bob Sorge, *Secrets of the Secret Place: Keys to Igniting Your Personal Time with God* (Lee's Summit, MO: Oasis House, 2001), 4.

I will study your commandments and reflect on your ways. I will delight in your decrees and not forget your word (Psalms 119:15-16 NLT).

There is an incredible difference between trying to grasp something with only one finger as opposed to two. In the same way, there is a huge difference in not only hearing the Word from a sermon but also learning to be alone with the Father and studying the Word for yourself. You have a wonderful opportunity to hear from God through His Word every day.

Throughout history, there has been a deception to the common person that reading Scripture was only for the priest or the pastor. This is due in large part to the fact until the last century, the majority of people couldn't read. In fact, throughout history, most things were taught orally rather than by print.

In addition, in the church, for almost a millennium, the only accepted translation of Scripture used in the Western churches was the Latin Vulgate.[3] At one time, many people understood Latin, but over the centuries most of the population lost that ability. Latin then became a language that only the educated, mainly priests, could understand. As a result, the sermons and

---

3. Coleman Ford, "The Catholic Versions of the Bible," ed. John D. Barry et al., *The Lexham Bible Dictionary* (Bellingham, WA: Lexham Press, 2016).

prayers performed in the Mass were spoken in Latin, and people would listen with no understanding.

Beginning in the late fourteenth century, a man named John Wycliffe translated the Bible into English from Latin because people didn't know Scripture.[4] In the sixteenth century William Tyndale translated the New Testament from Greek to English. Martin Luther translated the Bible into German.[5] Johann Gutenberg brought improved printing techniques to Europe so the Bible could be reproduced more easily. Around 1520, Jacob Lefevre translated the first French-language Bible. During the Marian Exile, Protestant reformers were determined to produce a Bible that the common person could study and understand. They created the Geneva Bible, which was the first to use numbered verses. The translators adopted the numbers supplied by the Stephanus Greek text of 1551 to make it easier to find passages of Scripture. This was the Bible that the Puritans brought to America.[6]

We live in a day where more than 550 languages have complete translations of the Bible. There are over 1,300 languages that have access to the New

---

4. Norman L. Geisler and William E. Nix, *A General Introduction to the Bible, Revised and Expanded* (Chicago: Moody Press, 1986), 547–548.
5. Guy P. Duffield and Nathaniel M. Van Cleave, *Foundations of Pentecostal Theology* (Los Angeles: L.I.F.E. Bible College, 1983), 41.
6. Michael Kuykendall, "Geneva Bible," ed. John D. Barry et al., *The Lexham Bible Dictionary* (Bellingham, WA: Lexham Press, 2016).

Testament.[7] Satan will do anything to keep God's people spiritually anemic. This is only possible if he can get you to rely upon someone else to tell you what God is saying. Despite all that is available to us today, it's still amazing how many believers think it is up to the pastor to read the Bible, and not for the common person. You must begin to study the Bible for yourself.

> For we do not wrestle against flesh and blood, but against principalities, against powers, against the rulers of the darkness of this age, against spiritual *hosts* of wickedness in the heavenly *places.* Therefore take up the whole armor of God, that you may be able to withstand in the evil day, and having done all, to stand (Ephesians 6:12–13 NKJV).

What if you were to head out the door for the day without getting dressed? How awkward and exposed would you be to the world? Of course, you would never do it. You know the predicaments in which you might find yourself. Have you ever thought about how important it is to get spiritually dressed before you go out the door? You would have left yourself exposed to the fiery arrows of the enemy and all the "wickedness in the heavenly places." That is why Paul says you must put on the full armor of God.

---

7. "Why Bible Translation — Wycliffe Bible Translators." *Wycliffe Bible Translators* (n.p., 2015), https://www.wycliffe.org/about/why, accessed December 11, 2016.

Think about the pieces of armor that Paul tells believers to put on. We are to wear the breastplate of righteousness. Who is our righteousness? Jesus! We are supposed to put Jesus on the front of us. Next is the helmet of salvation. Who is our salvation? Jesus! You are supposed to fill your mind with Jesus. The belt of truth—Jesus is the truth that holds you up. The shield of faith—our faith is in Jesus. The shoes of the gospel— Jesus is the gospel. The armor of God is Jesus. Don't go through your day spiritually naked. You need to be clothed in Jesus every day. Begin to study the Word for yourself.

A second finger makes quite a difference for grasping the sword of the Spirit. But you still need a better grip.

> Don't go through your day spiritually naked. You need to be clothed in Jesus every day.

Finger #3 — Study the Word with Others

And let us not neglect our meeting together, as some people do, but encourage one another, especially now that the day of his return is drawing near (Hebrews 10:25 NLT).

When my family and I lived in St. Louis, we would go down to the great Gateway Arch by the Mississippi River. You can always find a horse-drawn carriage to take a trip around the city. The horses that pull those carriages are Belgians. A Belgian horse can pull 8,000 pounds by itself. But two Belgians can pull 24,000 pounds—and if those two horses have worked and spent time together, they can pull 32,000 pounds. That is an exponentially larger load compared to doing it all alone.

It is incredible how much I learn from the Holy Spirit through others as I hear them pray and respond to the promises of God. In the first chapter, I wrote about how God created us in His image. One of the aspects of His image is that He made us for relationships. God created us to exist in spiritual communities, and incredible growth occurs when we invite others into our lives to challenge us as we grow. I have learned that my ability to grow and learn increases exponentially when I am in a group with other believers.

If you join a *Promise Principle* group, you will be amazed at how much God speaks to you through the prayers and responses of other believers. They become so encouraging that you won't want to miss a group time. A pastor from one of our campuses at Gateway Church once sent me an email that said:

"One of my group members called me last week before our meeting and told me that he wasn't going to be able to make it to group that week. He explained that he was going to be out of town on a hunting trip. He said that he hated to miss the group, and asked if it would be OK to call in. So before our group started, I called him and put him on speakerphone. He took part in our study on Ephesians 5. Afterward, he sent me a picture of him and his bow, following along on his iPad from the tree stand. I've been leading groups for a long time, but this was the first time I had somebody who wanted to be in the group so much that they listened in while hunting."

You have probably heard that there is no such thing as a "Lone Ranger" Christian. If you try to live that way, you will miss one of a believer's greatest privileges—the opportunity to walk with other people through Scripture, to be challenged by others, and to allow God to use you to teach others. Three fingers are even stronger than two are, but as you begin to respond to the promises of God, you will find that you need a grip that won't let go.

> If you try to live that way, you will miss
> one of a believer's greatest privileges—
> the opportunity to walk with other people
> through Scripture, to be challenged
> by others, and to allow God
> to use you to teach others.

Finger #4 — Memorizing God's Word

How can a young person stay pure?

By obeying your word.

I have tried hard to find you—

don't let me wander from your commands.

I have hidden your word in my heart,

that I might not sin against you (Psalm 119:9–11 NLT).

Purity means to be untainted or without fault. How
can you live a faultless life? Obey all of His promises—
every truth and commandment. The psalmist asks how
to avoid straying from the commands that he should
obey. The answer is by hiding them inside the center of
your heart through memorization.

If you immediately think that you can't do this because
you have difficulty memorizing, remember what I wrote
earlier. When you begin praying God's promises, you will
start memorizing Scripture with your spirit rather than

just your head. God tucks those promises down in your spirit as you pray them.

Why is hiding the Word of God within you so important? When temptation comes, you won't be able to say, "Time out! Let me go grab my Bible!" Trouble comes in real time, so you must immediately take that thought captive; you must be able to obey and avoid wandering from His commands. It has to be within you. Memorizing God's Word is the fourth finger, and it is connected to the fifth finger's ability to work. If you are doing these four things, your grip is very strong, but watch how strong your grip can really get.

Finger #5 — Meditating on God's Word

Blessed is the man
who walks not in the counsel of the wicked,
nor stands in the way of sinners,
nor sits in the seat of scoffers;
but his delight is in the law of the Lord,
and on his law he meditates day and night.

He is like a tree
planted by streams of water
that yields its fruit in its season,
and its leaf does not wither.
In all that he does, he prospers (Psalm 1:1–3 ESV).

179

The first psalm contains one of many promises that God will bless and prosper the person who meditates. If I could offer you a foolproof marketing plan for prosperity, how much would you pay for it? Psalm 1 has a plan for success that is free, and it is in the Bible. God promises prosperity to anyone who meditates on His Word.

Don't get off track with the word "prosperity." I am using it because the Bible uses it. It does not mean to achieve financial success. The idea in the Hebrew is of God putting His hand on you and pushing you forward. Would you like God's hand to push you forward in your spiritual journey, your relationships, and your ministry? Blessing comes when you meditate.

The nineteenth-century German evangelist George Müller was famous for his work among orphans. He wrote:

> I saw that the most important thing I had to do was to give myself to the reading of the Word of God, and to meditation on it.... What is the food of the inner man? Not prayer, but the Word of God; and .... not the simple reading of the Word of God, so that it only passes through our minds, just as water runs through a pipe, but considering what we read, pondering over it, and applying it to our hearts.[8]

---

8. Gary Rieben, *Give Me That Book: A Treasury of Truth for Troubled Times* (Enumclaw, WA: WinePress, 2013).

The definition of meditation is "to ponder, to give serious thought and consideration to selected information with an implication of speaking to review the material." When you prepare for an exam you memorize your notes and study them over and over again, so that when you take the test you can recall the material. Meditation on the material of Scripture helps you prepare for spiritual tests.

My dad grew up on a dairy farm. He taught us that cows like to chew something called the cud. As a child, I thought maybe that was their version of chewing gum. He explained that a cow in the field would start thinking about what it ate earlier in the day and think, "Hmm, that grass was really good! I think I will chew that again." The cow will regurgitate its meal and chew on it again. This helps the cow get more moisture and nutrients from the food.

When you not only memorize Scripture, but also spend time meditating on what you have previously hidden in your heart, you will have access to more spiritual food when you are in the middle of troubles or trials. If you don't have your notes memorized and you have not spent time meditating on them, you can't fully respond to the test. You can't respond fully to the promise of God in a particular circumstance if the promise isn't fully digested. This process is what James wants us to "continue in":

Anyone who listens to the word but does not do what it says is like someone who looks at his face in a mirror and, after looking at himself, goes away and immediately forgets what he looks like. But whoever looks intently into the perfect law that gives freedom, and **continues in it**, not forgetting what they have heard, but doing it—they will be blessed in what they do (James 1:23–25 NIV emphasis added).

You cannot count the benefits that come from meditating on the Word of God. The Lord told Joshua to meditate on it day and night and to obey it, and he would be prosperous and find success in everything he did (Joshua 1:8). You don't have to meditate only during your quiet time—you can meditate on Scripture while at work, at play, or any time. It's easy to neglect meditation in our busy world, but it has more promised results than any other spiritual discipline.

Thomas Brooks, a seventeenth-century English Puritan, wrote:

Remember that it is not hasty reading, but serious meditation on holy and heavenly truths, that makes them prove sweet and profitable to the soul. It is not the mere touching of the flower by the bee that gathers honey, but her abiding for a time on the flower that draws out the sweet. It is not he that reads most, but he that meditates most, that will prove to be the choicest, sweetest, wisest, and strongest Christian. [9]

---

9. Thomas Brooks, *Precious Remedies Against Satan's Devices* (Carlisle, PA: Banner of Truth, 1984).

Five Finger Review

Review the five fingers:

1. Hearing the Word of God.
2. Studying the Word for yourself.
3. Studying the Word with other believers.
4. Memorizing the Word.
5. Meditating on the Word.

If each of these disciplines represents a finger on your hand, what kind of grip do you have when you use all of them? If you only have two fingers currently, I encourage you to add another finger. Get into a Bible study with other people. If you have three fingers gripping the Word of God, add a fourth and start memorizing the Word. Wherever you are right now in life, I implore you to add these disciplines. Here is why you need them: If you hear the Word, study the Word by yourself, study the Word with others, memorize the Word, and begin to meditate on God's Word, you will find that you have saturated yourself in God's promises.

When you squeeze a wet sponge, whatever has saturated that sponge will come out. If you constantly grab hold of these things we have discussed, spirit and life (John 6:63) will come out when life's circumstances squeeze you.

In the image above, the first hand represents people who have saturated themselves with the Word of God. If you have this kind of grip, you automatically get to add the second hand. James 4:7 (NIV) says, "Therefore submit to God. Resist the devil and he will flee from you." This is a great promise. But you can't submit to something that you don't know.

When you look at the second hand, it doesn't seem like there is as much work on your part compared to the first hand. The lazy person might think, "I will just submit to God and have at least a one-handed grip. Then I don't have to do all the disciplines of saturating my life in the Word of God." But it simply doesn't work that way. Until you saturate your life in the Word, you won't be able to submit yourself to it. You will continue to wander away from God's commands. You won't be able to resist the devil. The enemy will not flee; he will simply come and

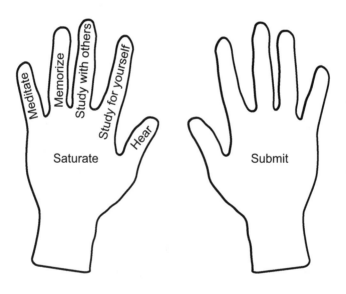

knock the sword right out of your hands. The enemy will forge weapons against you, and he will prosper rather than you.

How many fingers do you have gripping the Word of God? If God's promises are your weapon, how well do you grab your weapon? Are you grabbing hold of everything for which he has grabbed hold of you? I encourage you to add more fingers.

> Until you saturate your life in the Word, you won't be able to submit yourself to it. You will continue to wander away from God's commands.

12

Talk Is Cheap

For the Kingdom of God is not just a lot of talk; it is living by God's power (1 Corinthians 4:20 NLT).

Throughout this book, I have been writing about how we need to become spiritually mature. At the end of Chapter 1, I wrote that the initial experience of salvation must be followed by a process in which your spirit grows so that it can lead you, rather than allowing your body and soul to lead you. The Bible clearly says you can choose what will rule you. You no longer have to be a slave to sin. Righteousness can be your master. But you can't do this on your own power. In fact, that is impossible. You must let the Holy Spirit control you. Only then can you live as God wants you to live. You will never be able to do it on your own willpower. Talk is cheap. Many believers do a good job of telling everyone what they believe, but they live powerless lives. A Christian life doesn't emerge from a knowledge of Bible trivia. True life is possible only when the Holy Spirit rules in you.

> Talk is cheap. Many believers do a good job of telling everyone what they believe, but they live powerless lives. A Christian life doesn't emerge from a knowledge of Bible trivia. True life is possible only when the Holy Spirit rules in you.

Those who are dominated by the sinful nature think about sinful things, but those who are controlled by the Holy Spirit think about things that please the Spirit. So letting your sinful nature control your mind leads to death. But letting the Spirit control your mind leads to life and peace (Romans 8:5–6 NLT).

The Bible says quite clearly that if you let your flesh rule, the outcome will be destruction, but if you let the Holy Spirit lead, you will have life and peace. If given the choice of which door we want to walk through every person would choose the door of life and peace. Don't you agree? If this is true, what's stopping you? Why do so many Christians live defeated lives, not experiencing the life and peace that the Bible promises?

Discipleship Won't Work in the Flesh

I can anticipate the response that is coming: "I know that all God's commands are spiritual, but I'm not. Isn't this also your experience?" Yes. I'm full of myself—after all, I've spent a long time in sin's prison. What I don't understand about myself is that I decide one way, but then I act another, doing things I absolutely despise. So if I can't be trusted to figure out what is best for myself and then do it, it becomes obvious that God's command is necessary.

But I need something *more*! For if I know the law but still can't keep it, and if the power of sin within me keeps sabotaging my best intentions, I obviously need help! I realize that I don't have what it takes. I can will it, but I can't *do* it. I decide to do good, but I don't *really* do it; I decide not to do bad, but then I do it anyway. My decisions, such as they are, don't result in actions. Something has gone wrong deep within me and gets the better of me every time.

It happens so regularly that it's predictable. The moment I decide to do good, sin is there to trip me up. I truly delight in God's commands, but it's pretty obvious that not all of me joins in that delight. Parts of me covertly rebel, and just when I least expect it, they take charge.

I've tried everything and nothing helps. I'm at the end of my rope. Is there no one who can do anything for me? Isn't that the real question? (Romans 7:14–24 MSG).

189

Paul was a Pharisee who held to the strictest obedience of the law (Philippians 3:5). Yet, no matter how hard he tried, he couldn't do what he wanted because of his flesh. Even when he was doing his best, parts of his body would "covertly rebel." Can you relate to his confession? I certainly do.

There is no strategy for training your flesh to do the right thing. It is rotten to the core. For the rest of your life, a bad person will be within you, and it is you. Part of you can't be trusted. Your heart is deceitfully wicked and beyond any cure (Jeremiah 17:9). No matter how long you have been a Christian, your flesh will never change. It will not get better. This may be a piece of breaking news to you, but you cannot disciple your flesh. In fact, the older you get, the more rotten and sour your flesh will become. You have to hear this because you can't expect to just be in church your whole life and think that you can bypass your evil desires and make yourself a better person. Your flesh is beyond help.

> There is no strategy for training your flesh to do the right thing. It is rotten to the core. For the rest of your life, a bad person will be within you, and it is you.

Works of Your Flesh

Before you surrendered your life to Christ, your
spirit was completely dead. But God's Word promises
that when you trust Jesus' death on the cross for your
salvation and turn away from your sins, the Holy
Spirit comes into your life and your spirit is reborn
(John 3:1–7). You now walk with the Spirit—but before
the cross, your flesh always controlled you. And in
this broken and fallen world you had all kinds of experiences and places opened to the enemy where he
now has a foothold. You will uncover areas where you
aren't walking in the Spirit—areas that will hold you
in constant bondage. Consider some areas where your
flesh can be weak:

> The acts of the flesh are obvious: sexual immorality,
> impurity and debauchery; idolatry and witchcraft; hatred,
> discord, jealousy, fits of rage, selfish ambition, dissensions,
> factions and envy; drunkenness, orgies, and the like. I warn
> you, as I did before, that those who live like this will not
> inherit the kingdom of God. (Galatians 5:19–21 NLT).

Looking closer at this list, we can categorize them into
five areas:

1. **Sexual problems**: sexual immorality, impurity,
   debauchery (lustful pleasures)
2. **Spiritual problems**: idolatry, witchcraft (sorcery)

3. **Emotional problems**: hatred, discord, jealousy, fits of rage
4. **Relational problems**: selfish ambition, dissensions, factions, envy
5. **Substance problems**: drunkenness, orgies, and the like

We will all struggle with one or more of these areas at some time in our lives. I remember the first time I saw a crumpled page from a pornographic magazine. I was only 10 years old when I saw my first sex scene. (I was at a friend's house and we found a videotape under his father's bed.) There were times when I struggled with impurity in my dating relationships before marriage. There have been hundreds of moments in my life where I opened doors to the enemy in the area of sexual sin.

On the other hand, my parents didn't have alcohol in our home while I was growing up. My parents didn't drink, so it wasn't even something I saw when we were out at a restaurant. When I was 15 years old, I had a conversation with a woman in our church about her son; he had gone off to college, left his faith, and begun living a wild lifestyle, causing his family a lot of heartache. I had respected this young man when he was in high school, so I asked his mother why he was making these choices. She said her son claimed he had never seen anyone live without "sowing their wild oats" before surrendering everything to God. He said he was just building his testimony. To my knowledge, he never came back to the Lord. For some reason, God used that moment to make a deep impression on my heart. I wanted to be that one person who could live surrendered to Jesus. I had my struggles with sexual impurity, but I never drank or smoked in high school or college.

I have lived more than 40 years and I have never even tasted alcohol. I am not making a declaration about Christians and alcohol here. You should let the Lord convict you about that matter. But because alcohol never entered my life I have no desire for it. I can stand in a room filled with people drinking, and it isn't a temptation for me. What I consider "not a big deal" might be a much harder situation for a person with a drinking past. If you have had substance problems, your flesh is weak there, and it can cause destruction. My flesh has never had the opportunity to be weak in that area. Yet, because of my sexual past, I don't trust myself alone with a TV or computer if I am tired or spiritually weak.

When we are living through our flesh, working out of our experiences (whether by our choice or even because of wrongs done to us by someone else), we will struggle in one or more of these areas: sexual, spiritual, emotional, relational, and the misuse of substances. You need to examine your life and figure out where your flesh is weak and where the enemy will attack. I know where these places are in my life. Satan doesn't waste his time tempting me with substances or spiritual problems. There are other areas in my life, however, where my flesh is weak emotionally, relationally, and sexually. Yet, as I have learned to take everything captive and make it obedient to Christ, I have grown and had victory—but only to the extent to which I have given the Holy Spirit control of those areas of my life.

> You need to examine your life and figure out where your flesh is weak and where the enemy will attack.

It's All About the Spirit of God

There is therefore now no condemnation for those who are in Christ Jesus. For the law of the Spirit of life has set you free in Christ Jesus from the law of sin and death. For God has done what the law, weakened by the flesh, could not do. By sending his own Son in the likeness of sinful flesh and for sin, he condemned sin in the flesh, in order that the righteous requirement of the law might be fulfilled in us, who walk not according to the flesh but according to the Spirit (Romans 8:1–4 ESV).

Don't be condemned because of your flesh. Jesus fulfilled the righteous requirement of the law for each of us. You don't have to focus on wondering if you are righteous enough. Think on this. Suppose each of us has a "righteousness bucket" that we have to make 100 percent full. Every time you do a good deed—for example, walk in humility, keep a pure thought, live without any deceit, etc.—you get to put a little righteousness in your bucket. In this challenge to fill your bucket, your enemy is your flesh. Every time you were able to put a few drops in the bucket because of a good deed, your flesh would ruin it all by spilling the bucket. You cannot fill your "righteousness bucket."

So Jesus came to be a human exactly like us, but he had no sin. He became our perfect substitute. He filled our bucket of righteousness to overflowing. Paul says He fulfilled the righteous requirement in us (Romans 8:4). So you no longer need to worry about filling that bucket of righteousness. Jesus did it all. You are done. God is simply calling you to focus your mind on saying "Yes" to the Spirit. Our life as Christians is learning that it is all about the Spirit of God. Paul says in Romans 7 that it is impossible to live righteously; he then begins Romans 8 by saying that Jesus fulfilled righteousness for you and now you will walk in the Spirit by the power of the Holy Spirit. This theme runs throughout the New Testament.

Don't skip over these Scriptures; read them and meditate on them for a few moments:

> For those who live according to the flesh set their minds on the things of the flesh, but those who live according to the Spirit set their minds on the things of the Spirit. For to set the mind on the flesh is death, but to set the mind on the Spirit is life and peace. For the mind that is set on the flesh is hostile to God, for it does not submit to God's law; indeed, it cannot. Those who are in the flesh cannot please God.
>
> You, however, are not in the flesh but in the Spirit, if in fact the Spirit of God dwells in you. Anyone who does not have the Spirit of Christ does not belong to him. But if Christ is in you, although the body is dead because of sin, the Spirit is life because of righteousness. If the Spirit of him who raised Jesus from the dead dwells in you, he who raised Christ Jesus from the dead will also give life to your mortal bodies through his Spirit who dwells in you (Romans 8:5–11 ESV).

> But I say, walk by the Spirit, and you will not gratify the desires of the flesh. For the desires of the flesh are against the Spirit, and the desires of the Spirit are against the flesh, for these are opposed to each other, to keep you from doing the things you want to do. But if you are led by the Spirit, you are not under the law (Galatians 5:16–18 ESV).

Therefore do not be foolish, but understand what the Lord's will is. Do not get drunk on wine, which leads to debauchery. Instead, be filled with the Spirit (Ephesians 5:17 18 ESV).

You have two choices: Be filled with yourself or be filled with the Holy Spirit. If you think you can do what you need to do by being filled with your own self, you still don't know yourself very well. I know myself well enough to know that I can't do it by my own power. We must be filled with the Holy Spirit.

Please don't let that phrase confuse you. To be filled with the Holy Spirit doesn't mean that you are possessed. You have used this word yourself when you refer to someone being "full of themselves." It means that pride controls or consumes that person. To be filled with the Holy Spirit simply means that you are allowing Him, rather than your flesh, to control you. The flesh ruled our entire life before Christ, and rules much of our life even now. God saves us, and it is His will that the Holy Spirit will fill us and control us. This is why Jesus wanted His followers to teach others to obey everything He commanded (Matthew 28:20)—because everything He commanded is Spirit and life (John 6:63). In fact, it is obedience to what He commands—all that is Spirit and life—that allows us to be ruled by His Spirit.

> In fact, it is obedience to what He commands—all that is Spirit and life—that allows us to be ruled by His Spirit.

Suffocate the Flesh; Yield to the Holy Spirit

Those who belong to Christ Jesus have nailed the passions and desires of their sinful nature to his cross and crucified them there. Since we are living by the Spirit, let us follow the Spirit's leading in every part of our lives. Let us not become conceited, or provoke one another, or be jealous of one another (Galatians 5:24–26 NLT).

When the Holy Spirit rules in your life, it means you first have to crucify the flesh. Crucifixion is a serious matter. It involves understanding what your flesh deserves: a dramatic death. You can show no mercy. When the Romans crucified someone, death usually came by way of suffocation. After the criminal suffered several hours of torture, a soldier would break his legs. The criminal would no longer be able to pull himself up to inhale and would finally suffocate.

Crucifying the flesh means that you have to suffocate it. If you suffocate a flame, you don't allow it to get any oxygen. Without oxygen, a fire will die, no matter how strong it is. The areas in your life that cause you to struggle can't receive any more oxygen. I am not referring to your lungs: I am talking about the corrupt nature in you that is ungodly, selfish, wicked, and constantly trying to undo what God wants to do in your life. This isn't something you can casually approach if you are serious about yielding to the Holy Spirit.

When you pray, is this what your prayer sounds like? "Lord, I have this little anger problem. Would you help me not get so angry?" Imagine that you are driving your car, and someone in the passenger seat is acting insane. He is trying to get you to wreck your car. He grabs at the wheel and tries to steer you off the road. Do you put up with him because you feel somewhat sorry for him? If you do, he will kill you. That is exactly what your flesh is trying to do.

God wants to hear you say, "Lord, I am so unrighteous. I can't do this anymore with my flesh. Would you destroy it—take it out? I hate this old person in me! Crucify my sin. I put this flesh to death, and I don't give it any sympathy." How often do you need to say words like these? Frequently and every day! In prayer, "You also should consider yourselves to be dead to the power of sin and alive to God through Christ Jesus" (Romans 6:11 NLT).

How do you practice crucifying your flesh every day? You have to meet with God every morning and yield to the Holy Spirit. I am not saying you are supposed to make sure you have your "quiet time." If you think that way, you will get into a routine of just checking a Christian activity off your list. You need to get into the presence of God every morning, suffocate the flesh, and yield to the Holy Spirit. The Bible never says Jesus had a "quiet time." It does say He went off to a solitary place to pray and spend time with the Father. He did this to humble Himself and submit Himself to do and say only what He heard the Father say (John 12:49).

The reason you schedule time alone with the Father is to humble yourself and say, "I am not depending on me today. I am submitting myself to You to do only what I hear You say." You seek the presence of the Lord. You read His Word because it contains all the promises you need to walk in His nature rather than in your own. You are suffocating your flesh and yielding to the Holy Spirit. You are saying, "Holy Spirit, would You rule my heart, my eyes, my mind, and my actions today? Holy Spirit, I need Your help!"

> The reason you schedule time alone with the Father is to humble yourself and say, "I am not depending on me today. I am submitting myself to You to do only what I hear You say."

Jesus set the example; He didn't even have a sin nature that He needed to suffocate, but He still humbled himself before His Father. The Bible says He was "full of the Spirit," which means the Holy Spirit ruled and controlled him. He was not "full of the Spirit" simply because He was God. Yes, He was God, but the Bible says that He "emptied himself" (Philippians 2:7 ESV). No human can completely grasp what His self-emptying entailed, but Scripture says He took the form of a servant and was found in human likeness. He did everything fully in the power of the Holy Spirit. His Father enabled Him to do it. Jesus modeled this way to crucify the flesh so that we could follow His example. He expected us to follow His lead and share His expectations when He said, "I tell you the truth, anyone who believes in me will do the same works I have done, and even greater works, because I am going to be with the Father" (John 14:12 NLT). In Galatians it says He is going to the Father to send His followers the Holy Spirit:

> But the Holy Spirit produces this kind of fruit in our lives: love, joy, peace, patience, kindness, goodness, faithfulness, gentleness, and self-control. There is no law against these things! (Galatians 5:22–23 NLT).

How will you know if the Holy Spirit has control of your life? You will see the fruit of the Spirit overflowing in your life in every circumstance. When you face any temptation that is sexual or substance-related, you will see self-control and faithfulness. When circumstances attack you emotionally or in your relationships, you will see patience, kindness, gentleness, and even love. If you struggle with spiritual problems stemming from your past, you will see God's goodness and peace in your life. God wants these things for all of His children.

> Those who belong to Christ Jesus have nailed the passions and desires of their sinful nature to his cross and crucified them there. Since we are living by the Spirit, let us follow the Spirit's leading in every part of our lives (Galatians 5:24–25 NLT).

Crucifying the flesh and yielding to the Holy Spirit isn't just an idea that Scripture holds for a few spiritual leaders; it is God's mandate and expectation for every disciple. It is the believer's usual way of life.

Remember that Jesus took care of your sin problem by fulfilling righteousness for you so you don't have to live under the law. Stop focusing on trying to fill your "bucket of righteousness." Start putting all your focus on walking in the Spirit. God brought your spirit to life so you don't have to walk in the flesh. You just have to suffocate the flesh and yield to the Spirit.

Crucifying the flesh and
yielding to the Holy Spirit isn't just
an idea that Scripture holds for a few
spiritual leaders; it is God's mandate and
expectation for every disciple. It is the
believer's usual way of life.

13

Living Now for Eternity

Then God will give you a grand entrance into the
eternal Kingdom of our Lord and Savior Jesus Christ
(2 Peter 1:11 NLT).

In this final chapter, I will look at the entire reason
we should want to grow into spiritual maturity. At
the conclusion of Chapter 3, I wrote about experiencing
the "grand entrance into the eternal Kingdom of our
Lord Jesus Christ." When Jesus returns we will have
the opportunity to stand before our King and His throne
of grace. It will not be a throne of shame. There will be
no condemnation. We will experience a place where we
will give God all the glory for what He has done in and
through our lives—where we praise Him for His mercy
and grace. The focus will not be you or me. All attention
will revolve around the glory of God and the praise of
Jesus Christ. Yet, in this place all believers will give an
account for what they did or did not do.

> The focus will not be you or me. All attention will revolve around the glory of God and the praise of Jesus Christ.

For no one can lay any foundation other than the one we already have—Jesus Christ.

Anyone who builds on that foundation may use a variety of materials—gold, silver, jewels, wood, hay, or straw. But on the judgment day, fire will reveal what kind of work each builder has done. The fire will show if a person's work has any value. If the work survives, that builder will receive a reward. But if the work is burned up, the builder will suffer great loss. The builder will be saved, but like someone barely escaping through a wall of flames (1 Corinthians 3:11 15 NLT).

There is no other way for us to be saved, except by Jesus Christ alone. He is the foundation. A builder knows that the foundation is the most important part of a building. If the foundation is wrong, everything else—no matter how much it cost or how valuable the material—will all be wrong. Jesus is the only foundation for life, and no one can lay another foundation. However, Paul does say we are the ones who build on that foundation. On the judgment day what we have built on that foundation will be tested by fire. The materials that the builder has used will determine if the builder will receive a reward or will suffer great loss.

We can only choose from two types of building materials: eternal or earthly. Gold, silver, and jewels are eternal elements that will last forever. Hay, wood, and straw are earthly, temporal materials that fire will consume and decay will destroy over time.

Paul was not writing to non-believers. Only those who have put their trust in Jesus Christ have the foundation. Still, God will judge all believers for the material they have used. Have you continued to run after the things of this world? Do you live like those who are "shortsighted or blind, forgetting that they have been cleansed from their old sins?" (2 Peter 1:9 NLT). Or have you been discipled to walk in the Spirit and obey everything God has commanded? If you haven't, you may have the foundation of Jesus, but you haven't built with gold, silver, and precious jewels.

Only two things in this world are eternal: people and the Word of God. When God created people in His image, He made us eternal beings. He has even written eternity on every heart (Ecclesiastes 3:11). All the material things on this earth will be destroyed by fire. The only other thing on this earth that will last is the Word of God. Everything else will pass away, but the Word will last forever (1 Peter 1:25). Therefore, if you want to build on the foundation of Jesus with gold, silver, and jewels, you must invest your life in eternal things. Have you invested your life in the Word of God? Have you invested in the eternal purposes of people?

> So, dear brothers and sisters work hard to prove that you really are among those God has called and chosen. Do these things, and you will never fall away (2 Peter 1:10 NLT).

The apostle Paul says we are the Lord's workmanship, created to do good works that He prepared for us to do (Ephesians 2:10). He called us to live by His nature and to disciple others to live by it as well. God called us to respond to all of His promises and to lead others to respond to them. God called us to walk by the Spirit and to prove that we are really among those He has called and chosen.

If we follow the Lord's call the Bible promises that we will receive a reward. If we don't follow we will suffer loss. Fire will consume everything that isn't eternal. As believers, we will escape through the fire because Jesus is our foundation (1 Corinthians 3:15), but for eternity we will have nothing to show as evidence of our commitment to Him. However, that will not be the case for you and me. We will build on the foundation of Jesus with material that will last forever.

The Stories of Heaven

> Therefore, since we are surrounded by such a huge crowd
> of witnesses to the life of faith, let us strip off every weight
> that slows us down, especially the sin that so easily trips
> us up. And let us run with endurance the race God has set
> before us (Hebrews 12:1 NLT).

Imagine one day meeting the huge crowd of witnesses
in heaven. You are in the Great City talking with other
believers from all of history. Imagine meeting a Hebrew
man from the time of the Babylonian captivity. He was
never able to see his homeland or the temple, but he
believed in the prophecies of the coming Messiah and he
placed his faith in Yahweh. He asks you excitedly what
it was like to have Jesus the Messiah save you from the
power of sin and to have the Holy Spirit fill you. How
will you respond?

Imagine also meeting a Gentile woman from the
second century. Her grandfather had actually met Jesus,
and He healed her grandfather from leprosy. Their entire
family had put their faith in Jesus, but had to flee their
homes when Roman authorities slaughtered Christians
for confessing that Jesus, and not Caesar, was Lord. She
became a refugee, destitute and oppressed. She tells you
about the joy of dying in a coliseum, as lions mauled her
because of her faith in Jesus Christ. She is one of those
of whom the Bible says "the world was not worthy of

them" (Hebrews 11:38 NIV). She then asks with delight how you were able to live and suffer for the name of Jesus Christ. How will you respond?

Imagine meeting a man who lived during the sixteenth century. His father hired William Tyndale to be his tutor. Even though it was against the law to have the Bible in a language other than Latin, his mentor had translated it into English. This man treasured the Word of God, and his Bible was his most prized possession. Authorities arrested him and he was beheaded by decree of Queen Mary I. His Bible was dipped in his slain blood to warn others of his treachery. He then asks you with anticipation what passage of Scripture was your favorite to memorize and meditate on. How will you respond?

Imagine meeting a woman who lived during the early eighteenth century. Slave traders kidnapped her from Ghana and brought her across the ocean as part of the trans-Atlantic trade. A slaveholder purchased her on the auction block for $125 on her sixteenth birthday and she spent the remainder of her life as a slave. Other slaves on her plantation taught her about Jesus Christ. Though she never knew physical freedom and endured hard labor and mistreatment, she boasts to you about the freedom she found in Christ Jesus. She then asks you with joy about the freedom you enjoyed in Christ during your lifetime. How will you respond?

Imagine meeting a man named Aziz, who lived in Syria in the twenty-first century. He was empty and hopeless until one night a man in white appeared to him in a vision and told him that His name was Jesus Christ. He heard the gospel in the vision and surrendered his heart to Christ. He was a taxi driver. He would fill the trunk of his taxi with Bibles so he could give them to customers when he felt the Holy Spirit prompt him to share the love of the one true God. Several times, police pulled him over to search his taxi. Though the trunk was full of Bibles, they never found one. He was eventually betrayed by his brother-in-law, who was part of a terrorist group. They killed Aziz and his entire family. He then asks you boldly what you had to willingly give up to follow Christ. How will you respond?

Think about all the men and women who have gone before us. We have read about many of them in Scripture, but we will not hear the stories of the majority of them until we meet them in heaven. The thought of sharing my story one day with my brothers and sisters in Christ inspires me to run the race that has been marked for me.

The Finisher

We do this by keeping our eyes on Jesus, the champion who initiates and perfects our faith. Because of the joy awaiting him, he endured the cross, disregarding its shame.

211

Now he is seated in the place of honor beside God's throne (Hebrews 12:2 NLT).

You will hear millions of stories like those you just read. Like those people, you will want to run your race so that it is called "a life of faith." You may not live as a slave, you may not experience persecution or martyrdom, but you will face incredible circumstances in your life. Maybe you are going through difficult circumstances right now. "In this world you will have trouble" (John 16:33 NIV). The Bible says that you will have trouble, but it also says you can overcome by faith. Jesus ends that promise in the same verse of John's gospel by saying, "But take heart! I have overcome the world."

> You may not live as a slave, you may not experience persecution or martyrdom, but you will face incredible circumstances in your life.

Run the race by keeping your eyes on Jesus—by looking to your champion. He is the one who perfectly walked in faith. He is the one we want to follow. That doesn't mean the secret to living a godly life is merely asking yourself, "What would Jesus do?" You must fix your eyes on Jesus because He modeled the way to walk in faith. He responded to every promise, no matter what circumstances faced Him—even the cross.

> For all of God's promises have been fulfilled in Christ with a resounding "Yes!" And through Christ, our "Amen" (which means "Yes") ascends to God for his glory (2 Corinthians 1:20 NLT).

Jesus fulfilled every promise of God—every truth and commandment—with a resounding "Yes!" No matter what circumstance He faced, He walked in faith. Jesus perfected faith by acting on every promise of God. And our faith cannot be made perfect unless there is action on our part.

> Do you see that faith was working together with his works, and by works faith was made perfect? (James 2:22 NKJV).

The Greek word for "perfect" is *teleios,* which means to be made perfect, complete, fulfilled, or made to reach full maturity. Our faith matures or is made complete when we act on the promises of God. This action enables us to participate in His nature and not our own, which means we are allowing the Holy Spirit rather than our flesh to control us. Jesus responded to God's nature in this way. You might think, "But He was able to do that because Jesus already had God's nature." Yet if that were true, how could He be the finisher of our faith? He had to do it the same way that we have to do it. And we possess within us the same Holy Spirit that Jesus had.

God wants you to grow into maturity. He wants you to move beyond obeying what you feel or think in the circumstances of life. He desires that you would be obedient to His Spirit, so He has given you everything you need to walk in godliness. It's impossible to please God any other way. Continue responding to the promises of God. Continue learning to let the Holy Spirit lead you. Then one day we will get to be together in heaven and give our "Amen" for the life of faith we lived for God's glory.

"What we do in life echoes in eternity."

—Maximus[1]

> Continue responding to the promises of God. Continue learning to let the Holy Spirit lead you. Then one day we will get to be together in heaven and give our "Amen" for the life of faith we lived for God's glory.

---

1. Ridley Scott, *Gladiator* (Dreamworks SKG: 2000), Film.

Epilogue

But know this, that in the last days perilous times will come:
For men will be lovers of themselves, lovers of money, boast-
ers, proud, blasphemers, disobedient to parents, unthankful,
unholy, unloving, unforgiving, slanderers, without self-control,
brutal, despisers of good, traitors, headstrong, haughty, lovers
of pleasure rather than lovers of God, having a form of godliness but denying its power. And from such people turn away!
For of this sort are those who creep into households and make
captives of gullible women loaded down with sins, led away by
various lusts, always learning and never able to come to the
knowledge of the truth (2 Timothy 3:1–7 NKJV).

C urrently, in the West, we probably have more
resources and books than we could ever read. We
have magazines, commentaries, electronic applications,
and even computer software to help us understand the
Bible's original languages. Yet most of the church is still
spiritually immature and anemic in the knowledge of the
Word of God.

The apostle Paul speaks about how false teachers preaching false gospels will appear in the last days; and the people will not want to hear "sound and wholesome teaching," but only "whatever their itching ears want to hear" (2 Timothy 4:3 NLT). The prophet Amos refers to this time as "a famine of hearing the words of the Lord" (Amos 8:11 NIV). Amos doesn't say there will be a famine "of the words of the Lord" but of the actual hearing of the Word. How can we have so many resources, so much knowledge of truth that we can easily access, yet we live in a time Paul accurately described in 2 Timothy 3:1–7?

When we teach people about our *Promise Principle* discipleship groups, they often ask what material we are using. Our response is "The Bible." Their reply is usually, "Yes, I know, but what curriculum are you using?" We say, "The Bible!" The source must be the Bible. In fact, even this book you are reading now is only an aid—it isn't the source.

My hope and prayer is that this book has given you a new excitement about studying the Bible. I hope you have learned a new technique for reading Scripture—to not only read it and underline verses that you think are interesting, but also to interact with the Holy Spirit as you read. That means you are engaging your spirit through prayer as you learn to respond to all of God's promises. Your goal is to grow in spiritual maturity, so that your circumstances will no longer rule you, but rather the Spirit of God will rule—that you wouldn't merely have an outer appearance of godliness while failing to experience God's power in your life. My prayer is that you would be whole, guarded by His peace, and that no matter what season you walk through, you will communicate the gospel to everyone around you (Ephesians 6:15).

If you are interested in beginning a *Promise Principle* group in your church, your home, or your business, I have provided the following guide for facilitators who want to begin a group.

> The source must be the Bible. In fact, even this book you are reading now is only an aid—it isn't the source.

Promise Principle Group Guide

The group facilitator's job is not to teach the students, but to shepherd the group through God's Word. A good shepherd cares for those God has entrusted to him or her. Remember this as you facilitate the group with C.A.R.E. as your guiding acronym.

Connect (with God)

Begin your group with prayer, thanking God for these participants and asking Him to meet with you. "Teach us as we respond to all that you have for us." (2 minutes.)

Aim

We always want to point the group to the *Promise Principle*. The apostle Peter tells us we have all we need to live as godly people (2 Peter 1:3–4). God has given us all these promises; if we respond to them, it will add to our faith, it will allow us to be productive in our knowledge, and we can participate in His nature rather than our own sinful nature. So we respond to each promise by *receiving it with thanks or asking for it by faith!* (3 minutes.)

Respond (to the Word)

Each week, read one chapter aloud from a selected book of the Bible. Have each person read the next verse as you go around the circle. I recommend doing this so that every person is engaged in Scripture. However, be sensitive to those who cannot read or have great difficulty reading aloud. The goal is to engage, not to embarrass.

Have the members of the group underline every promise. When a person points out a promise, as the facilitator, ask if this is a promise *for which we should thank God* or one *which we should ask Him for by faith.* Then ask the person to share why this truth or commandment is something that requires a response. This practice allows the person to interact with Scripture at a heart level rather than just a head level. Then ask that person to take what has just been verbalized and pray it.

Through this format, people will be able to be vulnerable with things that are occurring in their lives; the Holy Spirit, God's Word, and other people in the group can minister to them. (45 minutes.)

The Holy Spirit will teach your group as members are praying or as they listen to one another. Ask the group to write down promises or truths the Holy Spirit speaks to them about during the study. God spoke these promises to them, and we want them to remember these promises and continue to pray them out in their lives. (5 minutes.)

Encourage

Encourage the group to continue in the Bible book you are studying and go through a chapter every day. They should underline promises or truths that they find and ask the Lord whether these are promises that they should ask for by faith or something that they should receive with thanks. We encourage the group to invite friends, telling them that they can just listen the first time. We really want the atmosphere of the entire hour to be filled with affirmation. Affirmation and a spirit of unity provide the perfect setting for the Holy Spirit to work powerfully in the hearts of the people in your group. (5 minutes.)

Coaching Tips for the Study

- When a group member explains an underlined truth or promise, let that person talk about it for a moment—that is how to process with the mind. Then ask the member how they should respond to that truth. We are teaching people how to engage their spirit with the Lord. This is where the truth becomes not merely information but leads to transformation.

- Sometimes you will need to press a little bit and ask your members if they are dealing with specific circumstances that they need to pray about or respond to with promises. You must help them and may need to lead with transparency in your own life.

- Engage those who don't talk. They are processing the whole time, and you need to give them space to verbalize these things. I will usually ask them near the end if a particular verse spoke to them. I will then encourage them to respond to it.

- Always give credit to the Holy Spirit whenever someone learns something. We are teaching them that the Holy Spirit is the one who guides us into all truth. The Spirit reveals much in God's Word through discussion and prayer. When something jumps up in a person's spirit so that the person thinks, "Oh, that is good," reinforce the understanding that the Holy Spirit spoke to this person's heart. Make sure the group member writes it down. I always say, "A dull pencil is better than the sharpest mind at recording the whispers of God."

- Allow your members to minister to one another. Many times a person will see something in Scripture that applies to someone else's circumstance. Let them pray for each other.